ANNE BRADSTREET: THE WORLDLY PURITAN

ANNE BRADSTREET:
THE WORLDLY PURITAN

An Introduction to Her Poetry

by

ANN STANFORD

BURT FRANKLIN & CO.

NEW YORK

Library of Congress Cataloging in Publication Data

Stanford, Ann.
    Anne Bradstreet, the worldly Puritan.

    "Selected bibliography of works by and about Anne Bradstreet"; p.
    1. Bradstreet, Anne Dudley, 1612?-1672—Criticism and interpretation.
I. Title.
PS712.S8   811'.1   74-22319
ISBN 0-89102-030-6

Frontispiece: Detail of a map of New England from William Hubbard's *Narrative of the Troubles with the Indians*, 1677.

To
LEON HOWARD
and
VIRGINIA JAMES TUFTE

PREFACE

The poetry of Anne Bradstreet has two claims upon the reader of American literature. The first grows out of her place as the earliest poet to produce a large body of original work in America; the second, by far the more important, comes from the high quality of the poetry itself. Hers is a voice which overleaps the limits of an age and speaks in fresh and vibrant tones of human concerns. In recognition of such timelessness at least one edition of her poems has been published or reprinted in each century of our history.

Given its place and merit, the poetry of Anne Bradstreet deserves the scrutiny of a full-length study, for her accomplishment becomes clearer in the light of the circumstances, both literary and ideological, under which she wrote. Her work is influenced, first of all, by the ideas circulated generally among all educated people of the late sixteenth and early seventeenth centuries, ideas of the nature of man and the universe and of politics that differ markedly from those we hold today. Beyond these, her work reflects the Puritan religious concepts with which she was thoroughly indoctrinated; it shows, too, a remarkable sensitivity to the forms and genres which she inherited from the Elizabethans and which were being developed by other seventeenth-century writers.

But above all, Anne Bradstreet's entire canon represents the struggle between the visible and the invisible worlds. Earth and the things of earth had on her a solid grasp. Though the spirit might point out the virtues of the unseen, Anne Bradstreet was always most conscious of the pleasures and rewards of earth—love, family, comfort, learning, fame. Even the harsh realities of the new world, this wilderness in which she made her home, were preferable to the gold and jewels of the invisible kingdom. Her argument was a constant one, conducted life-long; the voice of the world was never quite overwhelmed even in her most religious poems. In keeping with her long inner dialogue, most of her poetry takes the form of argument—in the early poems, between characters; in the later, between the two parts of herself. During the first half of her career, the world is clearly supreme; during the latter part, the invisible wins, but never a clear victory.

The poet's involvement in the world is symbolized by the wide range of forms in which she cast her writing and the influences we can see in them. Her range included the encyclopedic quaternions, rhymed history, metrical prayers, formal memorial eulogies, elegies of personal grief, political broadsides, Biblical paraphrases, love poems, meditative poems, and in prose, a personal journal and meditations. All these she wrote in "a few hours snatched from sleep and other refreshment," and all these she wrote in styles varied according to the purpose of each, as dictated by the literary decorum of her day. But though she was familiar with the general current of ideas and with the work of many of the then popular writers, she did not slavishly follow any master. She rearranged and synthesized the literary forms she encountered to serve her own purposes. Despite its roots in the baroque, her work is essentially pragmatic and realistic as befits a writer so admiring of the world. In part these qualities grew out of the poet's character. But they may also have come from her experience of the American wilderness, where, severed from the full impact of changing literary fashions, she developed her own responses to those events which touched her most.

Like other true poets, she enlivened the conventions she received, transforming them into a unique and vigorous instrument. But she did not use that instrument for small or temporary ends. Her work is very much a whole. This study aims to look at the whole body of her poetry as she encountered prevailing literary forms and fashioned them into a personal voice for an ever deepening argument between the world she knew and the promise of a greater world to come.

ACKNOWLEDGEMENTS

I am particularly indebted to Professor Leon Howard, emeritus of the University of California, Los Angeles, for his encouragement of my study of Anne Bradstreet. I am grateful also to Professor James E. Phillips and the late Professor Hugh G. Dick for help in the study of the English literary background of the seventeenth-century colonial writers, and to Professor Virginia Tufte of the University of Southern California for many suggestions. Professor Everett H. Emerson of the University of Massachusetts and Professor Paul Zall of California State University, Los Angeles, have been especially helpful in their enthusiasm and encouragement of my completion of this work. I wish also to acknowledge the help of Canon A. M. Cook of the cathedral at Lincoln, Lincolnshire, who shared his knowledge of Anne Bradstreet and the places she may have lived. My debt to the long line of scholars who have added to our present knowledge of Puritanism both in Old and New England and to the background of sixteenth- and seventeenth-century poetry is substantial. To attempt to list them all singly would add a bibliography to these acknowledgements.

Since I first began the study of Anne Bradstreet's poetry over a decade ago, interest in the poet has increased remarkably and two books have appeared devoted to her life and works. In 1965 Josephine K. Piercy, who had earlier won a solid place in the colonial field with her *Studies in Literary Types in Seventeenth Century America (1607-1710)* (New Haven, 1939), brought out her *Anne Bradstreet,* the first book to treat the poet and her career; and in 1971 Elizabeth Wade White's long awaited, definitive biography *Anne Bradstreet: "The Tenth Muse"* was published. I, along with all those interested in the colonial period, have reason to be grateful to

iii

these two authors who have brought to Bradstreet the serious consideration she has so long deserved. My own work on the poet has been conducted concurrently with some work of these two writers and has at times overlapped theirs. An earlier version of this book had been completed at the time Elizabeth Wade White's biography of the poet came out. Where I have added material based on her findings I have added notes to the text. My own thesis that Anne Bradstreet acted out the drama of Puritan tension between this world and the hope of the next has been partially expressed in several essays over the past years which have appeared in *The New England Quarterly, Early American Literature,* and in a chapter on Bradstreet in *Major Writers of Early American Literature,* edited by Everett Emerson (Wisconsin, 1972). I am grateful to those editors who have allowed me in the past to express my ideas on this poet. The present study puts forth my thesis as a whole and embraces my entire work on the poet to date.

The staff of the Library of the University of California, Los Angeles, have been most considerate over the years, and I am especially indebted to Frances Rose for many favors. Likewise, the staff at the Henry E. Huntington Library in San Marino and the Clark Memorial Library, Los Angeles, have graciously made their collections of rare books and pamphlets available. I have received generous help from Elizabeth Leigh Merrell of the Huntington Library Press. I am grateful also to the Library of California State University, Northridge, to the staff of the English Department of the University, and to Barbara Rosen for her painstaking typing of the manuscript. I would also especially like to acknowledge the work of Rose Shade, Research Assistant, who prepared a study of Anne Bradstreet's images, which form the background confirmation for some assertions made in this essay.

TEXTUAL NOTE

Anne Bradstreet's poems were first published under the title *The Tenth Muse*, in 1650, but she corrected them for publication in *Several Poems*, sometimes referred to as the second edition, published in Boston in 1678. The 1678 edition contains also poems found among the author's papers at the time of her death. John Harvard Ellis brought out the poet's complete works in 1867. He included the text of *Several Poems*, together with the contents of the Bradstreet manuscripts now in the possession of the Stevens Memorial Library at North Andover, Massachusetts. His edition contains an extensive introduction and notes; it remains invaluable to students of Anne Bradstreet. Two other good editions of Anne Bradstreet's poetry are available. A handsome "reader's edition" with modern spelling and punctuation, edited by Jeannine Hensley, was published by the Harvard University Press (Cambridge, Mass., 1967). Hensley based her text on a copy of *Several Poems* owned by the Massachusetts Historical Society; she includes in an Appendix all the variations in every available copy of that book. The Hensley edition is enlivened by two excellent essays, the "Introduction" by the editor herself, and a "Foreword" by the distinguished poet, Adrienne Rich. The need for an inexpensive edition has been filled by *Poems of Anne Bradstreet*, (New York, 1969) edited by Robert Hutchinson, which rearranges the poems but follows the text of the Ellis edition with corrections based on Hensley's study of the variant texts. Hutchinson also provides an excellent introduction and notes. Josephine K. Piercy has edited the reproduction of *The Tenth Muse (1650), and, From the Manuscripts Meditations Divine and Morall Together with Letters and Occasional Pieces by Anne Bradstreet* (Gainesville, Florida, 1965). The facsimile is reprinted from the copy of *The Tenth Muse* in the possession of Indiana University and the manuscripts in the Stevens Memorial Library. Piercy has in this book given the reader a chance to glimpse the appearance of those pages which brought forth from the poet the cry that at the press her "errors were not lessened (all may judg)." The reader may also see in these pages the author's bold hand and the blots and smudges which time, or the difficult quill pen, have added to the pages. All in all, Bradstreet has been well served by her twentieth-century editors.

Quotations from Anne Bradstreet's poetry in this book are mainly from the second (1678) edition, *Several Poems Compiled with great variety of Wit and Learning, full of Delight.* Where it has been necessary to quote from the first edition, *The Tenth Muse (1650),* I have identified the quotation by an asterisk (*). Work not in these two editions is quoted from the notebook in the Stevens Memorial Library as edited by Josephine K. Piercy.

The Chronology at the end of this volume identifies the place of first publication of all Anne Bradstreet's writing.

Readers following in the Ellis edition will note that Ellis does not give line numbers for the poems. The Hutchinson edition, based on Ellis, does number the lines. Readers using the Hensley edition will find a discrepancy between line numbers in Hutchinson and Hensley because the latter includes titles of poems in the line count while Hutchinson does not. Where I have given line numbers, I have not counted titles as lines.

CONTENTS

St. Botolph's Church, Boston, Lincolnshire, England, where Anne Bradstreet was a parish-
ioner before emigrating to the New World. Engraved from a drawing by J.M.W. Turner.

INTRODUCTION

As do all writers, Anne Bradstreet wrote in response to a vast web of experiences — those of an age and those uniquely personal. The elements of a particular time and place, of a particular sex and class, are intrinsic to various portions of her canon. Though her best poems open out to touch other human beings on a universal basis, they remain bound at many points to biography. Hence an acquaintance with the basic outlines of her life is necessary for any illumination of her poetry, at least on the first level of meaning.

Anne Dudley was born in 1612 or 1613 in Northamptonshire, England, where her father, Thomas, was clerk to the noted lawyer, Augustin Nicholls. Thomas Dudley and his wife Dorothy Yorke were well born — members of the gentry; and Thomas even claimed descent from the younger line of the aristocratic Sutton-Dudleys, an ancient family which Sir Philip Sidney was also proud to number among his ancestors.[1]

In 1619, when Anne was around six or seven, her father accepted the post of steward to the fourth Earl of Lincoln, and the Dudley family moved to the Earl's estate at Sempringham, eighteen miles from Boston, in Lincolnshire. At the time of the move the family included three children, the oldest, a boy, Samuel, then the daughters Anne and Patience. Later these were joined by three younger daughters — Sarah, Mercy, and Dorothy.

Boston, with Sempringham, lay in the plain surrounding that great indentation on England's eastern coast known as the Wash. The land was flat, somewhat resembling the Low Countries just across the Channel. Boston itself was a center for the wool-trade; the comparatively quiet waters of the Wash made it a haven for ships, which frequented the busy harbor. Boston was also a market town, with a fair which drew the inhabitants from miles around to gaze at the rich merchandise, "the Hats and Fans, the Plumes and Ladies tires," the "glittering plate and Jewels" later described by the poet,[2] as well as more common goods. The city was rich and important enough to support one of the finest parish churches in England, called St. Botolph's, after the saint from whom the town also took its name. And for twenty years, St. Botolph's had as its vicar, John Cotton, the most eloquent non-conformist preacher in England.

The manor house at Sempringham was on the site of an ancient priory taken from the church in the days of Henry VIII. The Earl also owned an ancient castle at Tattershall, and a town house in Boston, with a deer park which ran down to the river.[3]

The Earl was just nineteen or twenty when Thomas Dudley became the manager of his estates, and he had a number of younger brothers and sisters. His mother, the Countess, was somewhat ahead of her time, having written a book advocating that ladies of wealth should nurse their own infants, rather than give them over to wet nurses.[4] The high-spirited Earl was later to distinguish himself as one of the six lords who refused to pay the forced loan that King Charles demanded in 1628.

As a young person growing up in this liberal and enlightened household, Anne Dudley enjoyed the company of aristocrats and gentlefolk, people of education and leisure, who had the opportunity to read, listen to music, to dress well, and to enjoy whatever other amenities were available to the upper classes, including attendance at religious services in the Earl's own chapel. Sometimes these were conducted by leading non-conformist ministers, like Dr. Preston of Cambridge.

When Anne was about nine the company at Sempringham was enlivened by the addition of Simon Bradstreet, who, on the recommendation of Dr. Preston, became assistant to Thomas Dudley in the stewardship of the Earl's estates. This young man of twenty had just received the B.A. degree at Cambridge, where he had spent much time in the company of the Earl of Lincoln's brother. For a while during his stay at the University, Bradstreet had also been governor to the young Earl of Warwick, a son of Lord Rich by his first wife, Penelope Devereux, the "Stella" of Sir Philip Sidney's sonnets. From 1621 to 1624 Simon Bradstreet assisted Dudley at Sempringham. At the end of that time, he remained in charge of the Earl's affairs on the estate, while Thomas Dudley moved with his family to Boston. There the Dudleys could more easily listen to the preaching of John Cotton and to his lectures on Thursday afternoons. Perhaps on some of these occasions, Anne may have seen Anne Hutchinson, who often came from the town of Alford, twenty miles off, to listen to the preaching of the vicar. The family remained in Boston even after young Bradstreet left the service of the Earl of Lincoln to take a similar post in the household of Frances Wray, the Dowager Countess of Warwick, who had succeeded Stella as the second wife of Lord Rich.[5]

Sometime around 1628 Anne Dudley, then about 16 years old, became ill with the dreaded smallpox. We do not know whether others in the family were also stricken, but in any case, they all survived. Shortly after her recovery, Anne married Simon Bradstreet and went with him to live in the household of the Countess.

But the young matron was not destined to enjoy for long the luxurious life of a gentlewoman in one of the great houses of England. For plans were even then being made for the great migration which would sweep up many of the comfortable middle class gentry and set them down in a new and alien world. Boston, Sempringham, and the household of the Earl of Lincoln had together become a focal point of this phase of the Puritan movement. The members of the household represented several non-conformist families, including the father of the Earl's wife, Lord Saye and Sele, said by Clarendon to be "the oracle of those who were called Puritans."[6] The Earl's sister Susan was married to John Humphrey, one of the original patentees of the Massachusetts Bay grant. Another sister, Arbella, was the wife of Isaac Johnson, a wealthy landowner and active in the plans for emigration.[7] The family of

Bradstreet's other employer, the Countess of Warwick, was also a Puritan one. Lord Rich had been "zealous in religion";[8] his son, the second Earl of Warwick, was a leader among the Puritan lords and much interested in the colonization of America, being especially associated with the colonies in Massachusetts Bay and Connecticut.[9]

Since the accession of Charles I in 1625, the Puritans had encountered increasing pressures and disappointments. The new king's wife was a Catholic, and Charles supported the Arminian party within the Church, a group whose view that a person might achieve salvation through his own efforts seemed to the Puritans a heresy. Moreover, the new king had dismissed Parliament and in December, 1626, attempted to raise money by a forced loan. The loan encountered a spirited resistance among all classes. The Earl of Lincoln, together with the Earl of Warwick and four other Earls, refused to subscribe. Moreover, a member of the Earl of Lincoln's household prepared and published an abridgement of the English statutes for free distribution. The book was suppressed, and the Earl was proceeded against in Star Chamber. He was imprisoned in the Tower and confined there until March of 1628.[10] In March, 1629, Charles formally dissolved Parliament.

In an atmosphere of discouragement over the prospects of establishing a purified church in England, some of the Puritan leaders, including several of the Sempringham group, decided to leave the country. Among the emigrants were Thomas and Dorothy Dudley with their children, and Simon and Anne Bradstreet. By March, 1630, the group was ready. John Cotton went down to Southampton to preach the farewell sermon, and on April 8, the four ships of the fleet set sail. The ship *Arbella* carried the most prominent emigrants, including presumably the Dudleys, the Bradstreets, the Lady Arbella and her husband Isaac Johnson, and John Winthrop, the governor. The company arrived in the new world on July 12. According to Dudley they found the colony at Salem which was to prepare the way for them "in a sad and unexpected condition, above eighty of them being dead the winter before; and many of those alive weak and sick; all the corn and bread amongst them all hardly sufficient to feed them a fort-night. . . ."[11]

Most of the new immigrants soon left Salem for Charlestown, where a "great house" had been built by earlier arrivals. The Governor and several of the patentees lived in this house, while the rest "set up cottages, booths and tents about the Town Hill."[12] Illness and death plagued the new settlement. Some had arrived sick with scurvy, and others quickly became ill from lack of proper provisions and from the damp that seeped into the lodgings. The weather was hot; there was a lack of running water. By December, an estimated two hundred of those who had left England in April were dead.

The reaction of those who survived was one of shock. Thomas Dudley commented dryly that their predecessors "by their too large commendations of the country and the com-modities thereof, invited us so strongly to go on, that. . .we set sail from Old England."[13] And the poet herself later recalled her own rebellious feelings on first coming into the country: "I found a new world and new manners, at which my heart rose. But after I was convinced it was the way of God, I submitted to it and joined to the church at Boston."[14] In the spring of 1631 came another move, this time to Newtown, later called Cambridge. This town was well planned, with almost parallel streets, regular setbacks for the houses, and as William Wood noted, many "fair structures."[15] The Bradstreets did not re-main long in this pleasant village, however; around 1635 they moved on to the new frontier town of Ipswich, and ten years later, to the inland plantation of Andover. There Anne Bradstreet lived until her death in 1672. During these years she became the mother of eight children, all of whom grew to maturity. Her husband and her father and various other of her relatives played prominent roles in the government of the colony.

Thus with the poet we embark on a long pilgrimage, from the well-kept fields of England to the rocky and wooded and strange land of America, where, as in the words of Bradford, there were no "inns to entertaine or refresh their weatherbeaten bodys."[16] We find in her poetry not so much a description of the sea and land over which she passed as an account of the state of mind of the pilgrim. We follow her as she moves from rejection to acceptance of the new world as her home. And we find played out the drama that so intrigued the Puritans and their spiritual descendants, the struggle between the values of this world and the wonders of the invisible world toward which they made their way.[17]

PART I

THE IPSWICH POEMS

THE IPSWICH POEMS

From the early years of settlement there remains one poem by Anne Bradstreet, "Upon a Fit of Sickness, *Anno*. 1632," which gives the author's age as nineteen. The poet may have written it after emerging from the second hard winter in the new world, perhaps during the illness she recalled years later in her journal: "After some time I fell into a lingering sicknes like a consumption, together with a lameness, which correction I saw the Lord sent to humble and try me and doe mee Good: and it was not altogether ineffectuall." The poem contains thirty-two conventional lines on the imminence of death, the promise of heaven, and the shortness of earthly life. The meter is the ballad or common meter chosen by Sternhold and Hopkins for their popular translation of the Psalms.

Though its author mainly repeats ordinary seventeenth-century ideas, the poem claims our interest as Anne Bradstreet's earliest extant work, indicating some of the ways her poetry was later to develop. In theme it resembles one of her last poems, "As weary pilgrim," though the latter is much more mature and expresses a genuine world-weariness. It also foreshadows the poems of the later notebooks, in which Anne Bradstreet prays, or praises God for recoveries from various illnesses. Here she begins with the prospect of impending translation to a higher state:

> Twice ten years old, not fully told
>   Since nature gave me breath,
> My race is run, my thread is spun,
>   Lo here is fatal Death.

We feel here, in the simple statement that death threatens one so young, the beginning of the resentment more strongly stated nearly forty years later in the elegies on her grandchildren. In this, as in later poems, we notice the force of personal, rather than general, comment, the intrusion of a genuine persona into what might otherwise remain straight dogma. This intrusion, a hallmark of Anne Bradstreet's poetry, will give her later work, as it develops, a vitality that reaches beyond the poetic attempts of her New England contemporaries. Already in this early period she handles the difficult double rhyme with grace.

There are no reports of the poet's activities during the time she lived in Newtown to show whether she was writing other poems, though the facility she shows here indicates she had had some practice in versification.

Meanwhile the town grew, and the inhabitants began to feel the need for more land. In 1633 the General Court ordered that a settlement be made at Agawam, reported to be the best place in the land for farming and cattle, and John Winthrop, Jr., son of the Governor, was sent with a party of twelve men to begin the plantation, then "the most remote and isolated settlement" in the Bay, a walk of thirty miles by Indian trail from Boston.[1] In 1635, Thomas Dudley with his family, including Simon and Anne Bradstreet, and some of the other residents of Newtown moved to the new village, by then called Ipswich.

It was at Ipswich that Anne Bradstreet wrote most of her early work, including all the dated poems in her first book. The poems themselves suggest a stimulating intellectual environment. Isolated as the settlement was, it contained persons of means and education. The younger Winthrop, a man of unusual charm and ability, returned there in the fall of 1636, remaining for about three years. No doubt he brought his excellent library, which at one time contained over a thousand books. He was a genial and energetic man, projecting plans for salt-works and iron-works and new settlements. He had traveled to Italy and the near East, and during his lifetime corresponded with some of the most important men in Europe. Another early inhabitant of the town was the minister Nathaniel Ward, who had taken his M.A. at Emmanuel College, practiced law in London, and traveled extensively on the continent. With his pungent wit, he was much in demand as a preacher.

Richard Saltonstall, Jr., the son of Sir Richard Saltonstall, brought his young wife and child to the settlement in 1635. He was only a year or two older than Anne Bradstreet, and like her husband and Nathaniel Ward, had studied at Emmanuel College. As the scion of a nobleman, he was a leader in the town, owning the grist mill and serving as an assistant for several terms. Always outspoken, he raised his voice over such issues as a code of laws for the colony and the punishment of dealers in slaves. Another neighbor, Richard Bellingham, like the Bradstreets, came from Lincolnshire, where he had been recorder of his borough and the member of Parliament for Boston. Taking up his residence at Ipswich, he served as an assistant and several times as governor of the colony, but he is best known today for his brief appearance as the governor in Hawthorne's *Scarlet Letter*.

Also living in Ipswich were several members of Anne Bradstreet's own family. Her brother Samuel with his wife, the daughter of Governor Winthrop, lived there until 1637. And Anne's sister Patience, with her husband Daniel Denison, were permanent residents. Daniel Denison served over the years as town clerk and magistrate, assistant, deputy, speaker of the House, Commissioner of the United Colonies, and Major General of the colonial forces. Other prominent members of the community were the ministers Nathaniel Rogers and John Norton, the latter a pre-eminent scholar; John Whipple, elder of the Ipswich church; and Samuel Symonds, who later became deputy governor.

Several of these men were known in the colony as liberals. Bellingham, Bradstreet, Saltonstall, and Ward were often found on the side of the people in their increasing demands for more political power, and they were joined by others from Ipswich to protest when the government of Winthrop became too autocratic.

During the time the Bradstreets lived in Ipswich, the town grew from a small frontier settlement to the second largest town in the colony. There were craftsmen to supply the needs of the inhabitants — the records show a wheelwright, a cabinet maker, a butcher, a tailor, and others. Ipswich was apparently taking on some of the characteristics and its people were performing some of the services, that might be found in a small English town.

Thus, with some of the colony's best educated people, with libraries such as those of John Winthrop, Jr., and Thomas Dudley, in addition to the Bradstreet's own collection, with the liberal, and sometimes controversial, political atmosphere engendered by the Ipswich leaders, Anne Bradstreet must have found intellectual stimulation despite the remoteness of the town in which she lived. In addition, she found encouragement in her desire to write.

Doubtless she pleased her husband by her poems, many of which are addressed directly to him. But probably the person who most encouraged her in the early period was her father. The image of Thomas Dudley conveyed by many histories of the Massachusetts Bay Colony is that of a stern disciplinarian, and to religious dissidents "a whip and Maul." His daughter found his manners "pleasant and severe." But she also found him "known and lov'd, where ere he liv'd, by most," a "true Patriot," humble, mild, wise, and pious. He was a "devourer" of books[2] and wrote poetry himself. Several of Anne's poems are accompanied by notes to her father, and in her poem written in his memory, she calls him "Father, Guide, Instructer too."

Only one poem by Thomas Dudley has survived. Writing in tetrameter couplets he speaks of a readiness for death and warns his survivors against heresy. Another of his poems, now lost, portrayed the four parts of the world as four sisters arguing over their relative merits. Dudley's "sisters" no doubt served as model and inspiration for his daughter's quaternions. She says that the "view thereof did cause my thoughts to soar." In still another poem sent to her father with some verses she expresses her debt:

> Most truly honoured, and as truly dear,
> If worth in me, or ought I do appear,
> Who can of right better demand the same?

And she asks that he accept her poem in part payment. Undoubtedly she was sending her verses to someone who valued them. Though her claims are modest, the lines attesting her belief that her writing was worthwhile and her belief that others found it so served to bolster the dedication to poetry that we find throughout her work.

That her poetry was a source of pride for the whole family we may judge from the commendatory verses written by various relatives. John Woodbridge, the husband of her sister Mercy, was instrumental in having her *Tenth Muse* published in England. Both in the preface to the reader and in his commendatory poem he praises her poetry. The poem attributed to his brother Benjamin, who had lived for a short time at Andover while the Bradstreets lived there, asks men to "confess yourselves outdone." Another neighbor from Ipswich, Nathaniel Ward, likewise applauded her book, challenging Apollo to choose between it and that of Du Bartas.

Thus, during the years at Ipswich, Anne Bradstreet enjoyed the requisites of a stimulating intellectual life. The most important settlers in Ipswich were well-educated, leaders in the more forward-looking movements in the colony. There were books available — the libraries of John Winthrop, Jr., Thomas Dudley, and the Bradstreets themselves, together with the collections which such educated men as Norton, Bellingham, Ward, Saltonstall, and Nathaniel Rogers may have had. These books preserved for Anne Bradstreet the ideas and ideals of the great age of Elizabeth, which the Puritans could look back on in contrast to the reigns of the Stuarts. There were new ideas too, for visitors, new settlers, and new books continually arrived from England. And above all, there was approval of the poetry that Anne Bradstreet wrote and encouragement of her writing by the members of her own family, her husband, her father, and at least a few of her neighbors.

ILLVSTR. L.

Book. 4.

AN *Arme* is with a *Garland* here extended;
And, as the *Motto* faith, it is intended,
To all that perfevere. This being fo;
Let none be faint in heart, though they be *flaw:*
For, he that *creepes,* untill his *Race* be done,
Shall gaine a *Wreath,* afwell as they that *runne.*
This being fo; let no man walke in doubt,
As if Gods *Arme* of *Grace* were ftretched out
To fome fmall number: For, whoe're *begins*
And *perfeueres,* the profer'd *Garland* winns:
And, God refpects no perfons; neither layes
A ftumbling blocke in any of our Waies.
This being fo, let no man think't enough
To fet his hand, a little, to the Plough,
And, then defift; but, let him ftill purfue,
To doe that *Worke,* to which that *Wreath* is due:
For, nor on *Good-beginners,* nor on thofe
That, *walke halfe-way,* (much leffe on him, that goes
No ftepp at all) will God this *gift* conferre;
But, onely, unto thofe that *perfevere.*

　　LORD, by thy *Grace,* an entrance I have made
In honeft *Pathes;* and, thy affiftance had,
To make in them, fome flow *proceedings* too.
Oh grant me, full abilitie, to doe
Thy facred *Will;* and, to *beginn,* and *end*
Such *Workes,* as to thy *glory,* ftill, may tend.
That (*Walking,* and *continuing* in the *Path,*
Which evermore, thine approbation hath)
　　I may that *Garland,* by thy *grace,* obtaine,
　　Which, by mine owne *defert,* I cannot gaine.
　　　　Glory be to God.

Emblem from George Wither's *A Collection of Emblemes,* 1635.

CHAPTER 1
THE EARLY ELEGIES

Anne Bradstreet's public poetic career began with the composing of an elegy in praise of Sir Philip Sidney in 1638. Apparently she had just been reading the book titled *Du Bartas His Divine Weekes and Workes, with a compleat Collection of all the other most delight-full Workes Translated and written by the famous Philomusus Joshua Sylvester Gent.* , first published in 1621. Besides the long poems by Du Bartas, the book contained a number of poems by Sylvester himself that the young New Englander read with special interest. Among these were a group of memorial elegies on several private and public persons, which Sylvester had designed for presentation to the families of the deceased. Most of the elegies included a long eulogy in iambic pentameter couplets followed by one or two epitaphs, a common structure for memorial poems in the early seventeenth century.

No doubt Anne Bradstreet, who felt strongly attracted to her kinsman, Sir Philip Sidney, found special pleasure in a poem which celebrated that hero and also in a memorial poem addressed to Sir Philip's brother, Lord Lisle, on the death of his son Sir William Sidney. Sylvester's lines "Although I know none, but a Sidneys Muse,/Worthy to sing a Sidney's Worthiness" perhaps served as a challenge to the young poet. After all, in her veins ran that same Dudley blood of which Sir Philip had been so proud. Anne Bradstreet accepted the challenge in "An Elegie upon that Hounourable and renowned Knight *Sir Philip Sidney,* who was untimely slaine at the Seige of Zutphon, Anno, 1586," and she mentions their kinship, saying: "Let then, none disallow of these my straines,/Which have the self-same blood yet in my veines."*[1]

The poet's attempt at entry into the company of the immortals did not succeed. The poem swings wildly from topic to

9

topic, and the persons addressed by the would-be Muse include the Nine Muses as a group, Sidney himself, "noble Bartas," and the Stella of Sidney's sonnets. Along the way, she indulges in a number of complicated, drawn-out analogies, which stray far from the central subject. The passages of direct address are set within a narrative framework, thus forcing the poet to alternate between being narrator (using pronouns in the third person) and being a character in the action (addressing other characters directly).[2] Likewise, she falls into a difficulty still characteristic of the work of tyros, letting the tone vacillate uncertainly from serious eulogy to broadly comic humor. Anne Bradstreet, herself realizing that something has gone wrong, adopts the line which perhaps set her to writing in the first place, changing it to "But *Sidney's* Muse can sing his worthiness." Thereupon for the rest of the poem, she launches an attack on her own lack of ability; in a long digression she compares herself to that son of Apollo, Phaeton, who tried, and failed, to drive the chariot of the sun, and concludes by allowing the angry Nine to drive her off Parnassus.

The faults of this poem — its lack of unity and the over-working of the lengthy digressions — overshadow its virtues. Yet the poem has appropriate vigor in rhythm and choice of words, and some of the episodes by themselves — on Stella and on Phaeton, for example — are amusing as well. Although in this elegy Bradstreet's dialogue was inexpert, she was learning to handle it and would continue to use dialogue and argument, directly or indirectly, in much of her later work. Moreover, the elegy employs wit, somewhat in the manner of her mentors Sylvester and Du Bartas, in the elaborate analogies and the play on words ("Thus being over-come, he over-came"), though she never went to the extremes of either.

In 1641 Anne Bradstreet wrote an elegy on the poet Du Bartas himself. This time she has the poem completely under control — the tone is consistent; the digression — again it describes her own muse — contributes to, rather than distracts from, the whole. And in 1643, she wrote the third in the series, in "honour of that High and Mighty Princess Queen Elizabeth of most happy Memory." This elegy is more elaborate, with a proem, the poem itself, and two epitaphs, and it combines eulogy with history, feminism, and some sly political comment.

The political comment is subtle enough that its author did not remove it in the second edition after the Restoration. It is apparent only to those familiar with Sylvester's book, where in one of the poems dedicating the book to James I, he compares the newly crowned king to a phoenix risen from the ashes of its predecessor:

Our SUN did Set, and yet no NIGHT ensew'd;
Our WOE-full loss so JOY-full gaine did bring,
In teares wee smile, amid our sighes wee Sing:
So suddenly our dying LIGHT renew'd.
As when the ARABIAN (only) Bird doth burne
Her aged body in sweet FLAMES to death,
Out of Her CINDERS
A new Bird hath Breath,

In whom the BEAUTIES
Of the FIRST returne;
From Spicie Ashes of the sacred URNE
Of Our dead Phoenix (dear ELIZABETH)
A new true PHOENIX lively flourisheth,
Whom greater glories than the First adorne.
So much (O KING) thy sacred Worth presume-I-on,
JAMES, thou just Heir of *England's joyfull* UNION.

Bradstreet, replying to Sylvester's presumption, says of the departed Queen:

Since time was time, and man unmanly man,
Come shew me such a *Phoenix* if you can.

She goes on to deny the compliment to James:

She was a Phoenix Queen, so shall she be,
Her ashes not reviv'd, more Phoenix she.

The Queen remains more of a Phoenix dead than if her ashes are revived in the form of James I. Elizabeth, she says, is the

"Pattern of Kings," the "yet unparalled Prince." "Our Sun did Set, and yet no Night ensew'd," says Sylvester. "She set, she set, like *Titan* in his rayes," rejoins Anne Bradstreet, "No more shall rise or set so glorious sun/Untill the heavens great revolution." For her, as for other Puritans — especially in the 1640's — neither James nor Charles could be considered comparable to the great Queen.

The three elegies based on Sylvester differ from one another in purpose and in tone. That on Sidney begins as a eulogy, but eventually turns into a discussion of the poet's problems in versification, rendered in the form of a comic scene. The elegy on Du Bartas generally keeps to its purpose of setting forth the virtues of its subject, and its tone remains consistently serious. The elegy on Queen Elizabeth praises the Queen, but uses that praise for the purpose of political and social comment. Filled with numerous puns and plays on words, its tone is more witty than elegiac.

Despite these differences the elegies have several characteristics in common. Like Sylvester, Bradstreet uses iambic pentameter with strong end-line stops and couplet rhyme. The couplet was to be her favorite form, and with two exceptions, she used it in all the work we can be sure was written before 1650. Also like Sylvester, Du Bartas, and other metaphysicals, she combines high sentiment with homely images and indulges in long conceits, puns, and word play such as "She's Argument enough to make you mute" and "Since time was time, and man unmanly man." In all three elegies she employs the rhetorical device of "outdoing," in which a poet renders praise by comparing his subject favorably with famous examples. Thus Bradstreet shows Sidney outperforming each Muse in her own art and calls him "Achilles," "Hector," and "Scipio." Du Bartas brings more glory to France than her greatest kings; and Queen Elizabeth surpasses Semiramis, Cleopatra, and other great queens of antiquity.

All three elegies began as attempts to praise persons whom Anne Bradstreet admired. Inspired in the beginning by Sylvester's poems, she followed his form of memorial for those recently dead, even though those she celebrated had been

dead for a generation. Unlike Sylvester, however, Bradstreet
did not write these elegies to reconcile the living to their loss.
The epitaphs she found in the memorial poems of Sylvester
and others remain as vestiges of her models, but the poet ex-
presses no sorrow at the taking off of Sidney, Du Bartas, and
Elizabeth. Only the memorial form is left, and into it is poured
such remnants of the elegiac tradition as Anne Bradstreet
found usable.[3]

Following Sylvester, Bradstreet reduces the rout of nymphs,
dryads, satyrs, Gods, and demi-gods that inhabit the classic
pastoral elegy to a few allusions, mostly in the digressions of
the tribute to Sidney. Likewise in both poets the conventional
involvement of nature in the process of mourning is omitted.
In Sylvester the mourners are realistically seen as the various
classes in the state or the bereaved family. Bradstreet devotes
little attention to mourners. However, a few lines in two of the
elegies are concerned with them, and they are significant in the
light of the themes of honor and fame that rule all three of
these early poems. The elegy on Elizabeth says

> Thousands bring offerings (though out of date)
> Thy world of honours to accumulate.

It is possible that the offerings took the form of literary
tributes.[4] Certainly that is true in the elegy on Sidney where
"noble Bartas" deplores the death in "sad sweet verse."
Bradstreet declares that the bringing of such tribute added to
Bartas' own praiseworthiness, another indication that
Bradstreet took seriously the convention that both the subject
and the author of a memorial poem gain a worthy, often long-
lasting, monument. In the second edition Bradstreet joins the
name of "Phoenix Spenser" to that of Du Bartas. Spenser
presents Sidney's death

> in sable to his wife.
> *Stella* the fair, whose streams from Conduits fell
> For the sad loss of her dear *Astrophel.*

She refers, of course, to Spenser's collection *Astrophel*, and
the word "sable" stresses the fact that the tribute took the

form of a book, either printed in black type or on the black or
black-bordered pages sometimes used for memorial poems, or
perhaps it is an echo of a line in Sylvester "Of sobbing words a
Sable Webbe to weave."

The classical attitude toward the evanescence of life is pre-
sent in Sylvester. "What is firm beneath the Firmament?" he
asks in the elegy on Prince Henry. But it is present in Anne
Bradstreet only in the poem on Sidney:

> Ah! in his blooming prime death pluckt this rose
> E're he was ripe, his thread cut *Atropos*.

Likewise, both poets fail to emphasize the conventional cry
against death, which has so prominent a place in Spenser's
Astrophel. "The Mourning Muse of Thestylis" in that book
says:

> Ah dreadfull *Mars* why didst thou not thy knight defend?
> What wrathfull mood, what fault of ours hath moved thee
> Of such a shining light to leave us destitute?

And Stella cries out:

> ...why should my fortune frowne
> On me thus frowardly to rob me of my joy?
> What cruell envious hand hath taken thee away.

These dramatic statements contrast with Sylvester's treatment
in the elegy on Sir William Sidney, where the poet reveals an
awareness of the convention and explains why he does not
emphasize it:

> But, why of *Death* and *Nature*, rave I Thus;
> Another *Stile* (My LISLE) befitteth us.
> Another *Hand*, another *Eye*, directs
> Both *Death* and *Nature* in These high Effects;
> The *Eye* of Providence, the *Hand* of Power,
> Disposing All in *Order* and in *Hower*.

The good religious man can no longer complain against
Providence. Sylvester says much the same thing in his elegy on
Mrs. Hill where he compares death's taking the best to the
effect of a storm on the finest fields, then continues:

> O! Who so constant, but would grieve, and grudge
> (*If not a Christian*) at th' All-ordering Judge.

The specific denial of the classical resentment shows clearly that Sylvester is aware of the elements of the pastoral elegy. Bradstreet makes no attempt to express the resentment of death or to follow Sylvester in his necessary religious resolution. But in her later work, in the tender elegies on her grandchildren, she will suggest, though she does not state, the resentment, and she resolves the poems in the manner suggested by Sylvester in the elegy on Sir William Sidney.

More important in these early elegies than the cry against death is the handling of the apotheosis, where the subject of the verse is translated to a higher sphere, to some sort of immortality. Such a translation is present in Sylvester's poems on Prince Henry, Sir William Sidney, and Mrs. Hill. In the Bradstreet elegies, the apotheosis is also present, but it is found in the promise of fame, not in a Christian transformation. Thus the Sidney epitaph concludes in the first edition:

> *His praise is much, this shall suffice my pen,*
> *That Sidney dy'd the quintessence of men.**[5]

The Du Bartas elegy elaborates the theme:

> Thy haughty Stile and rapted wit sublime
> All ages wondring at, shall never climb.
> Thy sacred works are not for imitation,
> But Monuments to future Admiration.
> Thus *Bartas* fame shall last while starrs do stand,
> And whilst there's Air or Fire, or Sea or Land.

The idea of fame permeates the entire elegy on Elizabeth, which begins

> Although great Queen thou now in silence lye
> Yet thy loud Herald Fame doth to the sky
> Thy wondrous worth proclaim in every Clime,
> And so hath vow'd while there is world or time

and continues on the note of fame and glory to the final epitaph.

The emphasis in all these poems is worldly glory. There is an increasing tendency to make the apotheosis of the subject through fame the principal theme of the poem. Nor is it that fame in heaven which Milton in "Lycidas" was able to justify. The elegies contain no references to the Bible or to religion at all. Fame is for Mistress Bradstreet, in these early poems, more important than Christian redemption. In this her elegies are closer to classical than to Puritan models. Moreover, the poet reveals in them her own desire for the fame that might be acquired through writing.

The elegies demonstrate both a method and a program by which she would work toward the poet's crown. Over and over again she was to take a current genre, emphasizing certain of its customary elements, and turn it into a personal form in which she as the poet often plays a central role, as in the first two elegies, or in which certain points are made which are personally important, as in the elegy on Elizabeth. In the Sidney and Du Bartas elegies, the digressions on the writer's lack of skill, which contemporary theoreticians encouraged as a means of developing amplitude, take over an exceptionally large number of lines. In fact, her "expression of inadequacy" becomes a theme uniting the poems, revealing to the reader the poet's own motives and aspirations. The poet wholeheartedly accepts the conventional and oft-repeated idea that poets make their subjects live in fame and that poets who so immortalize their subjects will themselves endure. Thus in rendering her praise of Sidney and Du Bartas into rhyme, Anne Bradstreet sees herself reaching for the Parnassus of the immortals.

In selecting the attributes for which she will praise Sidney, she emphasizes his literary achievements, especially the *Arcadia*, finding in that work the virtues other writers ascribe to the *persons* of their subjects — "learning, valour and morality,/Justice, friendship, and kind hospitality." And, in a later poem, she confesses envy of the "sugar'd lines" of Du Bartas. Most of the first fifty-four lines of the ninety-two line poem on the French writer are devoted to her own muse and her reaction to Du Bartas' accomplishments. Though she does

not refer to herself so often in the elegy on Queen Elizabeth, it
is evident that the Queen represented to the poet, and to the
world as well, the proof that women could reason well enough
to write. The Queen, in fact, excelled her masculine counter-
parts, being "so good, so just, so learn'd, so wise" that "from
all the Kings on earth she won the prize."

Moreover, the first two elegies reveal Bradstreet's program
for becoming a poet. She will arrive at her goal through ad-
miration and persistence. She is conscious of her own lack of
skill; yet she goes on anyway:

> So proudly foolish I, with *Phaeton* strive,
> Fame's flaming Chariot for to drive.*

Though she is laughed at by Apollo and driven from Parnassus
by the Muses, her own muse returns in the long digression of
the Du Bartas poem in the more modest guise of a child.
Knowing that "wishes can't accomplish my desire", she
enters that poem with a determination to continue in the art of
poetry:

> But barren I my Dasey here do bring,
> A homely flour in this my latter Spring,
> If Summer, or my Autumn age do yield,
> Flours, fruits, in Garden, Orchard, or in Field,
> They shall be consecrated in my Verse,
> And prostrate offered at great *Bartas* Herse.

This is the first dedication of the self to belles-lettres to be
written in New-England. The dedication grew out of Anne
Bradstreet's high regard for poetry as a "consecrated" art.
Even though she disclaimed any attempt to write that highest
form, the epic, she could at least strive in the more homely
genres. Such is the personal strand that runs alongside the out-
ward themes of praise for those great public figures of the
elegies. And through the garlands of verse she promised to
make in their honor, she hoped to gain her own small wreath
of fame and worldly remembrance.

Emblematic figure from Herman Hugo's *Pia Desideria*, 1624, showing a woman as a fountain of tears, and copied in Quarles' *Emblemes*.

CHAPTER 2
THE POEMS TO HER HUSBAND

Anne Bradstreet had small patience with the Petrarchan convention in which a poet adores his lady from afar. Her attitude is shown in the comments on the relationship of Astrophel and Stella in *The Tenth Muse*. Taking the sonnet series as biography, she admits surprise that such a paragon as Sidney should have languished so long in the unrequited love of a lady:

> O Princely *Philip,* rather *Alexander,*
> Who wert of honours band, the chief Commander.
> How could that *Stella,* so confine thy will?
> To wait till she, her influence distill,
> I rather judg'd thee of his mind that wept,
> To be within the bounds of one world kept.*[1]

For Anne Bradstreet, the ideal love finds its consummation and continuation in marriage.

The importance of marriage for her as for all Puritans, was increased by the belief in the family as the basic unit of government in both the state and the congregation. Especially in New England the state was considered to be made up of families, who were expected to exercise control over their members. Thus marriage was important to the state, but essential to marriage was love. God had commanded man and wife to love one another; hence the duty to love was a part of the marriage contract. Though marriages were usually arranged by Puritan families on the basis of social rank, young people were not forced to marry where they felt love would be impossible.[2] That a tender relationship was achieved among many Puritan couples is attested by such writings as the letters of John Winthrop to his wife, Thomas Shepard's references to his wife in his *Autobiography*, and the poems Anne Bradstreet wrote to her husband. Four of these are love poems. The first, twelve lines titled "To my Dear and loving Husband," comes as close to being a sonnet as anything Anne Bradstreet wrote. But it rhymes in couplets and the syntax is simple and direct, without the involution of phrase or meaning to be found in most sonnets. The other three are letters "to my husband, absent upon Public Employment." Since they bear the same title, I shall distinguish them by terms prominent in them, as the "Ipswich," the "Phoebus," and the "Loving-hind" poems.

Just as, thematically, the poems express a love exactly opposite to the Petrarchan ideal, so the methods, characters, and imagery differ. Here is no oxymoron, no freezing while burning, as in the Petrarchan conceits, but a straightforward analogy — the author is cold when her husband is away and warm when he is there, regardless of the season. Neither lady or love is idealized or distant; rather the marriage is happy in its consummation. This is stated and repeated in such lines as:

> If ever wife was happy in a man,
> Compare with me ye women if you can.

> I wish my Sun may never set, but burn
> Within the Cancer of my glowing breast,
> The welcome house of him my dearest guest.

> Tell him, the countless steps that thou dost trace,
> That once a day, thy Spouse thou mayst imbrace;
> And when thou canst not treat by loving mouth,
> Thy rayes afar, salute her from the south.

The Petrarchan love poem tended to blend with Neo-Platonism, and the final outcome of Petrarchan love was the approach to heavenly or ideal beauty through a series of steps beginning with physical love. For the Puritan, such an approach to heavenly beauty was not possible.[3] Love was not used for the purpose of striving for ideal beauty, since the ideal was to be achieved by other means — the regenerate heart was given the power to see the "beauty of holiness" and the world as an expression of God's glory. The Puritan attitude toward love was more utilitarian. Married union was a near necessity.

Love, both for Puritans and many other Elizabethans, when consummated by marriage, was to issue, not in aesthetic appreciation, but in the procreation of children. From the *Epithalamion* of Spenser, which closes with several references to fertility and procreation as the hoped-for outcome of the joys of the wedding night, to Milton, who couples marriage and procreation in the lines "Hail wedded Love, true source/ Of human offspring," the theme recurs. Nor does Anne Bradstreet divorce her love for her husband from a consciousness of love's utilitarian functions. In the Ipswich poem she says "In this dead time, alas, what can I more/ Then view those fruits which through thy heat I bore?" Here married love, while treated metaphorically, is nevertheless approached in a straight-forward, almost sensuous manner.

The four lyrics are bound together around a central idea — the union of husband and wife and the insistence on that unity despite physical separation. The first poem states the theme: "If ever two were one, then surely we." The Ipswich poem continues, inquiring "If two be one, as surely thou and I,/ How stayest thou there, whilst I at *Ipswich* lye?" The poet addresses her husband as Sol and begs him to return northward; while he is in the south, the day is too long. In the Phoebus poem she reflects this idea in the first line ("*Phoebus* make haste, the day's too long, be gone") before proceeding to ask the sun to carry a message to her husband. The Loving-hind poem, which compares the poet to a hind, a dove, and a mullet, repeats the idea which concludes the second poem of the series ("I here, thou there, yet both but one") by stating "I here, he there, alas, both kept by force" and ends by asking him to return so they may browse at one tree, roost in one house, glide in one river. Its last line echoes the first line of the first poem by "Let's still remain but one, till death divide." Thematically, then, the poems are closely knit. The expression of sorrow over separation controls them as each moves toward the conclusion that the division should be ended by the reunion of the spouses.

The linking of the love poems by reiteration of a common theme illustrates a practice Bradstreet followed in several genres. The early elegies, for example, though written at different times, coalesced around the theme of fame, heightened in each case by the central technique of showing the subject outdoing other great figures. Later, "Contemplations" and the personal elegies, written as successive pieces of a long work or as single poems, were to be connected by central themes. Bradstreet's poetic canon shows a remarkable wholeness. Themes and images recur, often controlling the structure of all the poems in a single genre, or like the concept of the four elements, being repeated as motifs throughout her work. The four poetic letters to her husband, are the most conspicuous example of Bradstreet's ability to unify separate pieces of her work, but the tendency persists throughout.

Within the letters themselves, movement occurs by a method characteristic of other lyrics of the late sixteenth and early seventeenth centuries, when poetry was considered a branch of rhetoric. The rhetorical oration was classically divided into three types: The demonstrative, fitted for the praise or dispraise of persons, places, or things; the deliberative, which was for the purpose of persuasion or exhortation; and the judicial, for use in argument on a question.[4] The deliberative method was frequently used in love lyrics, where the argument might take the form of comparisons or metaphors, not necessarily realistic. Fanciful arguments were often chosen as being more persuasive, and, in a poem like Donne's "The Flea," they became even fantastic.[5] Such strained arguments do not attempt to express experience directly. Rather they transform experience into a series of analogies or metaphors and explore the relationships among the analogies. The three letters of Anne Bradstreet were all written with the ostensible purpose of persuasion. Their method is not to describe realistically the state of her mind, but to move her husband by a series of arguments. Puttenham in his discussion of "that form of Poesie in which amorous affections and allurements were uttered" comments on the appropriate language for love poetry: "it requireth a forme of Poesie variable, inconstant, affected, curious and most witty of any others." Anne Bradstreet's language and metaphors in general

conform to the rules of poetic decorum described by
Puttenham. Certainly these love poems are the most "curious
and witty" of her work.

Various images in the love poems show an acquaintance
with those current in the literature of the time. The presence of
the same metaphors in poems by other authors does not
necessarily indicate a direct influence, however, since so many
writers drew upon the common store. The general tenor of
Anne Bradstreet's metaphor "I like the earth this season,
mourn in black,/ My Sun is gone so far in's Zodiack," for ex-
ample, is close to that in Donne's letter "To Mr. I.L."
Bradstreet's lines in the Loving-hind poem:

> Or as the loving Mullet, that true Fish,
> Her fellow lost, nor joy nor life do wish,
> But lanches on that shore, there for to dye,
> Where she her captive husband doth espy

may be based on a similar passage by Du Bartas in "The Fifth
Day." A "hartlesse deare" roams in the ninth line of *Colin
Clouts Come Home Againe*, and one pair of couplets used in
the Phoebus poem has its basis in the exaggerated tear im-
agery of the period:

> Tell him here's worse then a confused matter,
> His little world's a fathom under water,
> Nought but the fervor of his ardent beams
> Hath power to dry the torrent of these streams.

Such torrents of tears are found scattered throughout English
poetry of the late sixteenth and early seventeenth centuries.[6]
Anne Bradstreet has here ingeniously woven the tear imagery
into her central metaphor of sun-husband, earth-wife.

There are also some echoes of Biblical language in the love
poems. In the Phoebus poem Bradstreet refers to Genesis
22:17, saying: "He that can tell the starrs or Ocean sand,/ Or
all the grass that in the Meads do stand;" she also takes from
Genesis "flesh of thy flesh, bone of thy bone" in the Ipswich
poem. The central idea of the wife addressing the husband

may be related to the dialogue between the bride and bridegroom in the Song of Solomon.

The three love letters may have been written between 1641 and 1643,[7] a period of high poetic excitement for Anne Bradstreet. Possibly she wrote them soon after the re-reading of Du Bartas in 1641, for they represent her closest approach to the use of exaggerated comparisons. By the time she wrote another poem to her husband a few years later, she had completely abandoned the "witty" style and adopted the more direct manner of her later poetry.

The language of "Before the Birth of one of her Children" is completely straightforward. Writing with great seriousness, the poet suggests that she may die in the coming childbirth. She asks her husband to forget her faults and remember what virtues she may have had, and to protect her little children from "step Dames injury." She is aware that life is fleeting but she also says

> love bids me
> These farewell lines to recommend to thee,
> That when that knot's unty'd that made us one,
> I may seem thine, who in effect am none.

It was the Puritan belief that a marriage was dissolved at death. Marriage was for the earthly life only, and in any after life any union between spirits was no longer in effect.[8] Perhaps partly for this reason the regenerate spirits in Wigglesworth's poem *The Day of Doom* (stanzas 195-201) could watch without a quiver while their spouses, children, or parents went down to everlasting hell. God had said that a person must not love any earthly thing inordinately, and even excessive grief for a departed spouse was contrary to God's command. Anne Bradstreet voiced the Puritan view when she spoke of untying the knot "that made us one," just as she expressed it in the last line of the Loving-hind poem, "Let's still remain but one till death divide." But she tries to get around the idea of the complete severance of death by writing lines so that "I may seem thine, who in effect am none." She wants to be remembered.

Admitting that her husband will probably marry again, she still hopes that

> if chance to thine eyes shall bring this verse,
> With some sad sighs honour my absent Herse;
> And kiss this paper for thy loves dear sake.

Further, she requests him

> when thou feel'st no grief, as I no harms,
> Yet love thy dead, who long lay in thine arms.

In its emotional content, the poem — one of Bradstreet's several farewells to the world — tries to gain for its author earthly continuance in the memory of the living. In the earlier love poems, also, the poet attempted to circumvent the finality of death. Throughout, they reflect a love that goes beyond the merely rational and dutiful. "To my Dear and loving Husband" ends:

> Then while we live, in love lets so persever,
> That when we live no more, we may live ever.

The turn of phrase here reminds us of Cavalier poetry, though the lines themselves are ambiguous. They may mean that the loving couple will produce descendants, so that they may live on in their line. Or the couplet may mean that the two will become famous as lovers and live on in that fame. And the fame will come in part through the exertions of Anne Bradstreet's muse.

Such might be the whole import of these lines had they been based completely on the commonplaces of Renaissance sonneteers. But the intensity with which the Puritans focussed on grace and divine love adds religious overtones to this poem. The word love is played upon. As Saints, the lovers must persevere in the consciousness of the divine love within the covenant of grace in order to live ever. The love between husband and wife in the ideal state of marriage may be considered an analogy for the love between Christ and the soul or Christ and his Church. So the "Argument" preceding the Song of Solomon in the Geneva Bible explains: "In this Song,

Salomon by moste swete and comfortable allegories and parables describeth the perfite love of Jesus Christ, the true Salomon and King of peace, and the faithful soule or his Church, which he hath sanctified and appointed to be his spouse, holy, chast and without reprehension." Even so, the ardor with which Bradstreet addresses her husband in this "sonnet" and the three love poems threatens to overshadow a proper love of God by placing so high a value on one who is a mere creature.

What may have set the poet free to write so sensually of earthly love may have been her reading of *Sions Sonets* (1625) by Francis Quarles. In his book Quarles paraphrases the Song of Solomon in the form of an elaborate dialog between the Bridegroom and the Bride, who represent Christ and his Church. The "sonnets" take the form of eight-line stanzas rhyming in couplets. Quarles' language elaborates on the already sensuous imagery of the original; it includes puns, comparisons, and conceits prominent in the Renaissance. Though Bradstreet did not take whole phrases from Quarles' *Sonets* there are enough likenesses in imagery and tone to suggest that she may have daringly turned from reading the dialog of the heavenly Bridegroom and his Bride to write of her own earthly love in similar terms. In doing so, she transferred the image of the heavenly groom to Phoebus, the sun, and she herself became the earthly bride. Later in "Contemplations" she used the same imagery to describe the sun who "as a Bridegroom" from his "Chamber rushes." Later still she would unite the Bridegroom and the Redeemer in the final triumphant line of her valedictory poem "A Pilgrim." But this was still Bradstreet's early period when she concerned herself predominantly with the things of this world.

A poem written some years later, in 1658, repeats the themes of remembrance and poetic dedication. Though not written directly to her husband, it is a family poem, an expression of pride in the progeny which the couple has produced. From the first line, "I had eight birds hatch'd in one nest," throughout the poem, Mistress Bradstreet refers to herself and her children as a family of birds, narrating what has happened to each of her children, giving them advice, and expressing affection.

The imagery here is less dense and strained than in the love letters,[9] in line with the trend of her later poetry toward a more direct relationship between the experience and its expression. Despite the bird analogy, the emphasis is on human actions and feelings. In the quaternion on childhood, the poet gave a realistic picture of the young mother coping with the trials of raising children; in this poem the mother in her mid-forties gives voice to the very real love and concern of most parents for their offspring. Bradstreet is especially fine in her expression of the common hope that by precept and example, parents may teach their children solid virtues which remain as a legacy, so that "Thus gone, amongst you I may live."[10] Besides the exaltation of the abstract good that descends from parents to children, generation after generation, the poet asks for personal remembrance:

> When each of you shall in your nest
> Among your young ones take your rest,
> In chirping language, oft them tell,
> You had a Dam that lov'd you well.

Perhaps after the illness recounted in the notebook of 1656-1657, she realizes she is beginning to grow old — "My age I will not once lament/ But sing, my time so near is spent" — and she draws her most pleasing picture yet of the "country beyond sight,/ Where old ones, instantly grow young" in an eternal spring. Even in that far land she will continue to sing; she will "there with Seraphims set song." And she renews her dedication to earthly singing:

> Mean while my dayes in tunes Ile spend,
> Till my weak layes with me shall end.
> In shady woods I'le sit and sing,
> And things that past, to mind I'le bring.

Thus on the note of love, remembrance, and dedication, the poet closes the cycle of poems to her husband and family. In the series she has spoken again of the fame her muse sought in the early elegies, and she has added to it love and remembrance as goods to be desired and actively pursued in this world.

CHAPTER 3
THE QUATERNIONS

In her four long and important early poems, known as the quaternions, Anne Bradstreet celebrated the world itself, with all its creatures, including man. Once more the impetus for her verse came from Sylvester's book. And it came also from the poem by Thomas Dudley on the four parts of the world.

Anne had recently read or re-read her father's poem, in which he presented the four parts of the world as sisters who disputed over their claims to wealth, arts, and antiquity. She replied with two poems also about four sisters — the four Elements and the four Humours. These sisters, she good-naturedly reminds her father, in a letter sent to him with her poems, might "claim precedency" over his. They also engage in a spirited debate over precedency among themselves. She would have said more in her poem, she says in the accompanying letter "but fear'd you'ld judge one *Bartas* was my friend.*[1]

In selecting the subject for her poem, however, she may have had in mind a passage in which Du Bartas related the four quarters of the world of her father's poem to the characters in her own. Du Bartas wrote:

> Feeling the fower Windes, that with divers blast,
> From the fower corners of the World doo haste;
> In their effects I finde fower Temp'raments,
> Foure Times, foure Ages, and foure Elements.
> Th' *East-winde*, in working, follows properly
> Fire, Choler, Summer, and soft Infancy:
> That, which dries-up wilde *Affrick* with his wing,
> Resembles Aire, Blood, Youth, and lively Spring:
> That, which blowes moistly from the *Western* stage,
> Like Water, Phlegme, Winter, and heavy Age:

29

> That, which comes shiv'ring from cold Climates solely,
> Earth, withered Eld, Autumn, and Melancholy.[2]

Du Bartas' poem, however, employed straight description. The idea of a dispute among characters was suggested by the poem of Anne's father and probably also by another translation in Sylvester's book, the "Panaretus" of Jean Bertault, which told of a quarrel among four virtues.[3] Even so, the form of argumentative monologue came readily to the poet. She had attempted persuasion in the love poems, written about the same period, and her earliest elegy had been, as we have seen, in alternating narration and direct address. Argument, monologue, and dialogue continued as major ingredients in Anne Bradstreet's verse. And in the early work, the monologue and argument were frequently humorous. The humor was intentional: with it she attacked her own muse in the Sidney elegy; with the humor of metaphysical conceits, she urged her husband to come home in the love letters. In the quaternions, especially in the first two, each of the eight characters displays her wit at the expense of her sisters. The Elements and Humours take part in a boisterous, and sometimes hilarious, family quarrel. And we should at least note here that Anne herself was the oldest of five sisters.

It is the humor that enlivens the poem, that furnishes the "delight" by which poetry was supposed to teach. The humor is scattered here and there through "The Four Elements," most noticeably in the opening lines of "Water," but becomes most evident in the sarcastic undercutting of one Humour by another.

The sisters who quarrel in the first two quaternions and the procession of allegorical figures in the "Ages" and "Seasons" do not speak in a haphazard manner, however. Each speaks in turn and according to the appropriate rules of rhetoric. Each develops arguments from the form of the demonstrative oration, which holds up a person, city, country, or other subject to praise or blame. In the case of a person, the first point in an oration of praise should be the subject's distinguished ancestry, and Anne Bradstreet at the beginning of the second quaternion gives the "high descent" of each Humour from her proper Element. Likewise, she introduces the Four Ages by their "pedigrees" in the procession that begins their poem, and Spring and Summer identify themselves by their descent as soon as they appear.

In the case of a non-personal subject, such as a country or some other thing worthy of praise or blame, the oration should consider its physical aspects, its advantages and disadvantages, its uses and resources. These points form the framework for the arguments of the characters of the quaternions. Each discusses her or his physical qualities, advantages or uses, and disadvantages or power to do ill. An exception occurs in the spirited argument of the Humours, where each gives herself only praise, leaving a description of her less worthy qualities to the others. The poet shows she is aware of the change in oratorical form when she remarks in the introductory letter

> My first do shew, their good, and then their rage,
> My other four, do intermixed tell
> Each others faults, and where themselves excell.*4

Looked at in the light of rhetoric, the quaternions become a series of sixteen demonstrative orations delivered by the Elements, Humours, Ages, and Seasons about themselves.

The substance of the orations, especially in the first two quaternions, reflected the physical and metaphysical system of the four elements which had been originally conceived by the Greek philosophers. With Christian ideas added, the system remained as the basic cosmology of the Middle Ages and the Renaissance. Briefly, the Earth, formed of the element earth, hung at the center of the universe. Around the Earth circled an orb of water, then a globe of air. Beyond air stretched a circle of celestial fire. The elements tended to remain separate. However, they combined in various proportions to form the living and non-living beings of the earth.

The elements were frequently in conflict, particularly those set farthest apart in the celestial orbs.5 Bradstreet uses the conflict in a dramatic manner to begin her poem:

> The Fire, Air, Earth, and water did contest
> Which was the strongest, noblest and the best,
>
> .   .   .   .
>
> Whence issu'd winds & rains, lightning & thunder
> The quaking earth did groan, the Sky lookt black
> The Fire, the forced Air, in sunder crack;
> The sea did threat the heav'ns, the heav'ns the earth,
> All looked like a Chaos or new birth:
> Fire broyled Earth, & scorched Earth it choaked
> Both by their darings, water so provoked
> That roaring in it came, and with its source
> Soon made the Combatants abate their force
> The rumbling hissing, puffing was so great
> The worlds confusion, it did seem to threat
> Till gentle Air, Contention so abated
> That betwixt hot and cold, she arbitrated.

Once more she has precedent for this in Du Bartas, who describes the same quarrel, though in his version both air and water act as appeasers.

The elements are linked by their attributes of being hot or cold, moist or dry. Du Bartas speaks of the linking as a Maypole dance of the elements, going around hand in hand.[6] Anne Bradstreet uses the same figure to close her second quaternion, which is the last that deals with the subject of cosmology, and which comprised the ending of the original pair. Flegme concludes:

> Let Sanguine, Choler, with her hot hand hold,
> To take her moyst, my moistnesse wil be bold;
> My cold, cold Melanchollies hand shal clasp,
> Her dry, dry Cholers other hand shal grasp;
> Two hot, two moist, two cold, two dry here be,
> A golden Ring, the Posey, *Unity*.*

By beginning with the quarrel of the Elements in the prologue to the first quaternion and proceeding to the figure of Unity at the end of the second, Anne Bradstreet brings the original conflict to a conclusion in keeping with accepted ideas and at the same time gives an adequate structure to her poem by working from strife to the resolution of strife in the final figure.

In places during their quarrel the sisters speak of the encroachment of new ideas upon the little world of medieval cosmology. The old theories regarding the four elements were undergoing attacks from various quarters. Adherents of the new Copernican astronomy, though not yet in the majority and though specifically rejected by Du Bartas,[7] had questioned the old theory of the encircling spheres and the earth-centered universe. As a general rule, the Puritans were interested not so much in the ability of the new theory to explain heavenly phenomena in a simpler manner as in the effect of the two theories upon theology. The Copernican theory could not be accepted until it proved that it could be reconciled to dogma. Once this could be shown, the Puritans had no reason to hold to the Ptolemaic universe.[8] Bradstreet indicates that the old theory has been called into question. As Air, she says:

> I grow more pure and pure as I mount higher,
> And when I'm throughly rarifi'd turn fire:
> So when I am condens'd, I turn to water,
> Which may be done by holding down my vapour.
> Thus I another body can assume,
> And in a trice my own nature resume
> Some for this cause of late have been so bold
> Me for no Element longer to hold.

Not only had the element of air been under attack, but also the element of celestial fire:

> The Sun an Orb of fire was held of old,
> Our Sages new another tale have told.

Du Bartas vigorously objected to those who strove to cut away the element of fire, and Donne in "An Anatomie of the World" (1611) regarded the challenge to the old geocentric universe as one more indication of the progressive decay of the world. Du Bartas, too, speaks of the decay and its basis in man's original sin.[9] There is no such pessimism in Anne Bradstreet's "Four Elements."

The poem is practical rather than theoretical. Fire describes her uses in making tools, in touching off cannon and other explosives, in the smithy, in making kitchen implements and cooking food and so on. She briefly mentions celestial fires and lists various constellations: the *theory* of meteors is passed over to be described by the "wise." In the case of the other Elements also, the practical aspects are given in most detail, and the theoretical aspects ignored or only lightly touched on. The poet's comment about the sun is a factual statement. She cites her own experience to controvert the idea that the sun is not an orb of fire. Fire says:

> But be he what they will, yet his aspect
> A burning fiery heat we find reflect
> And of the self same nature is with mine
> Cold sister Earth, no witness needs but thine:
> How doth his warmth, refresh thy frozen back
> And trim thee brave, in green, after thy black.

This testing by her own experience is perhaps the strongest indication that Anne Bradstreet has been affected by the new philosophy. Experiment and observation, rather than reliance on authority, are the important elements of the new attitude. Here Anne Bradstreet supports old authority, but does it by the technique of observation.

She also brings into the poem a characteristic skepticism. When she speaks of the Phoenix, she adds "if any be." She mentions alchemy, but again with doubt; Fire says:

> And you Philosophers, if e're you made
> A transmutation it was through mine aid.

When her method is compared with that of Du Bartas, the difference becomes apparent. He gives the theory of natural phenomena, draws moral and religious conclusions, employs numerous classical characters, and includes mythical beasts along with actual ones. Anne Bradstreet displays greater plainness of style. She includes few figures of speech or puns and almost no classical figures. The work tends to rational explication or simple cataloging of the subjects she discusses. And Anne Bradstreet does not moralize.

Despite the differences, "The Four Elements" is closer to Du Bartas in style and content than any of Anne Bradstreet's other poems. Her mention of Du Bartas in the prologue to this work and her use of some of the same material covered by him in his *First Week* is probably the basis for the appellation she was given by her former neighbor Nathaniel Ward, who called her "a right Du Bartas girl"; and commentators from the Duyckincks on have tended to emphasize her indebtedness to the French writer. Du Bartas, however, was only one source on which she drew in her eclectic fashion. Her next quaternion, "The Four Humours," was more strongly influenced, at least in content, by the work of Dr. Helkiah Crooke.

In the second quaternion the subject of debate is the theory of humours by which man's vital processes are explained. The four Humours who take part in the debate are aligned with the four Elements who have already spoken; they represent in the little world of man the same forces that the Elements represent in the larger world.

Briefly, the theory of humours is this: food, made up of the four elements, is taken into the stomach, whence it goes to the liver, which converts the food into four liquid substances called *humours*. The four Humours are Choler, Blood, Melancholy, and Flegme, and they are the moisture of the body.[10] Each of them reigns over a particular organ. In Anne Bradstreet's poem, the heart is the seat of Choler:

> I in his heart erect my regal throne,
> Where Monarch like I play and sway alone.

According to Helkiah Crooke, in his anatomical treatise *Microcosmographia or a Description of the Body of Man*, the vessels that arise out of the liver "do minister nourishment to the whole body, wherefore the liver is called the shop of sanguification or bloud-making."[11] Hence, Blood praises the liver for giving nourishment and being benign. The spleen was well known as the seat of Melancholy, and Choler recognizes this when she addresses that Humour:

> Thou canst not claim the liver, head nor heart
> Yet hast the Seat assign'd, a goodly part

> The sinke of all us three, the hateful Spleen
> Of that black Region, nature made thee Queen.

Melancholy also claims the bones as well as the earthy parts of
man's body,[12] and she reminds the other Humours of her
relation to the element Earth. Flegme rules the brain, which is
the seat of the Soul, as well as most of the nerves.

The Humours also generate vital heat, which is carried
through the body by three kinds of spirits. The natural spirits
are generated in the liver and travel through the veins. In the
heart they are acted on by the heat and air from the lungs and
are transformed to vital spirits, which travel through the
arteries. In the brain they are turned into animal spirits, which
move through the nerves to execute the commands of the
brain.[13] The theory of the spirits is referred to by Dr. Crooke
where he discusses the reason why the proportions of the liver
are larger in man than in animals. It is because "it must make
bloud for the use of the whole body; not only for his nourish-
ment, but also to serve for his expence of spirits: for there are
more functions of the soul in a man, then in any other
creature; which functions spend more animall Spirits, and
those are engendred of the vitall spirits, and the vitall spirits of
bloud."[14]

Anne Bradstreet's Choler refers to the spirits; it is her heat
that

> . . .rarifies the intellectual parts:
> From whence fine spirits flow and witty notions:
> But tis not from our dull, slow sisters motions:
> Nor sister sanguine, from thy moderate heat,
> Poor spirits the Liver breeds, which is thy seat.
> What comes from thence, my heat refines the same
> And through the arteries sends it o're the frame:
> The vital spirits they're call'd, and well they may
> For when they fail, man turns unto his clay.
> The animal I claim as well as these,
> The nerves, should I not warm, soon would they freeze.

Blood claims the natural spirits in answering Choler:

And if vital Spirits, do flow from thee
I am as sure, the natural, from me:
Be thine the nobler, which I grant, yet mine
Shall justly claim priority of thine.

Flegme ascribes the animal spirits to the brain: "The Spirits animal, from hence do slide."

Bradstreet, further, follows the conventional description of the brain as given in Dr. Crooke's chapter on the subject. He divides man's faculties into faculties of sense, faculties of motion, and principal faculties. Of the faculties of sense, there are two kinds — external, involving the five senses, and the internal, or common sense. After this inward "sensitive faculty" follow the "principal faculties" of imagination and fancy, intellectual power, and memory. Dr. Crooke discusses the opinions of various authorities regarding the location of the soul and concludes in agreement with Philo:

> Wheresoever the kings Guard is, there is the person of the King whom they do guard; but the guard of the Soul, that is, all the organs and and instruments of the senses are placed in the head as it were in a Citadell or Sconce; there therefore doth the Soul keep her Court, there is her residence or Estate. If therefore the sensative faculty be placed in the brain, the Intellectuall must be there also, because as saith the Philosopher the office of the Intellectuall faculty is to behold and contemplate the Phantasmes or Images which by the Senses are represented unto it. We resolve and conclude therefore that the brain is the seat of all the Animall faculties as well Sensative as Principall.[15]

Anne Bradstreet, conforming to the ideas of Crooke, describes the brain with its three powers:

> Within this high Built *Cittadel*, doth lye
> The Reason, fancy, and the memory.

Also "the five most noble Senses here do dwell." She locates the sensitive soul in the brain:

And surely, the Soul sensitive here lives,
Which life and motion to each creature gives.

Her theory here, like that of Dr. Crooke[16] and other writers
such as Sir John Davies in his popular *Nosce Teipsum* (1599),
is that the soul has three powers: the vegetative, which it shares
with all living things; the sensible, which is shared with other
animals, and the rational, found only in man. She refers to this
hierarchy also in the lines: "What is there living, which do'nt
first derive/ His Life now Animal, from vegetive." Just as
does Davies, she mentions a higher soul than the sensitive one,
though she does not identify it as the rational soul. It is dif-
fused throughout the body, but she finds that it chiefly resides
in the brain:

> That Divine Offspring the immortal Soul
> Though it in all, and every part be whole,
> Within this stately place of eminence,
> Doth doubtless keep its mighty residence.[17]

Having finished with the brain's high functions, Mrs.
Bradstreet discusses the other parts of the body related to
Flegme. She mentions the marrow of the backbone and the
nerves and then says:

> Some other parts there issue from the Brain,
> Whose worth and use to tell, I must refrain:
> Some curious learned *Crooke*, may these reveal
> But modesty, hath charg'd me to conceal.

Crooke reveals:

> all the nerves, even the Opticks themselves, doe arise
> from this *Cerebellum*, or backward Brain, which me
> thinks *Hippocrates* insinuated in his Book *De
> Ossium Natura.* . .(saith he). . .*The Originall of the
> Nerves is from the* Occipitium *or hinder part of the
> Head, even to the Rack bones, the Hips, the
> Privities, the Thighes, the Armes, the Legs and the
> Feet.*[18]

Anne Bradstreet's modesty here is interesting in the light of
nineteenth-century criticism, particularly that of the
Duyckincks in their *Cyclopaedia of American Literature*:
"The good lady must have enjoyed the perusal of Phineas
Fletcher's *Purple Island*, a dissecting theatre in a book, which
appeared in 1633. Her descriptions are extremely literal. She
writes as if under bonds to tell the whole truth, which she does
without any regard to the niceties or scruples of the im-
agination."[19]

Anne Bradstreet's four Humours touch upon several other
theories of Renaissance physiology, two of which are par-
ticularly curious. One was in regard to the proportion of
elements contained in a particular body. Since the elements
were in a state of constant war, the most lasting bodies were
those in which the elements were compounded most equally.
Animals have shorter lives than men because the elements are
less well mixed in them.[20] Blood refers to this theory when she
says:

> Your hot, moist, cold, dry natures are but four,
> I moderately am all, what need I more;
>
> . . . .
> Nay, could I be, from all your tangs but pure
> Mans life to boundless Time might still endure.

Blood is also confirming the prevalent theory that the sanguine
man is nearest perfection.[21]

Mistress Bradstreet refers at another point to one of the
theories concerning disease. When any of the humours became
dried out through excessive heat, it was considered in an
"adust" state, which was dangerous to health, since the fumes
from the burnt humour might ascend directly to the brain and
cause frenzy or madness. Any adust humour might then
assume the name of "melancholy adust."[22] The humour
Melancholy refers to this in her lines addressed to Choler:

> When by thy heat thou'st bak'd thy self to crust,
> And so art call'd black Choler or adust,
> Thou witless think'st that I am thy excretion.

All in all, the allusions contained in the "Four Humours"
cover a wide range of theories of physiology current in the
Renaissance and earlier. Ellis states, though without giving
evidence, that "it is almost certain that she obtained her
wonderfully exact description of human anatomy from the
'curious learned Crooke.' "[23] Her reference to Crooke within
the poem and the numerous instances in which she closely
follows his work confirm Ellis's statement. In speaking of the
brain, she refers to Galen and Hippocrates, authorities con-
stantly quoted in Crooke's *Description*. The other suggested
source for the "Four Humours," Phineas Fletcher's *Purple
Island*, does not contain so many parallels. It is possible that
both these works used Crooke as a common source.

Here as elsewhere, however, Mrs. Bradstreet did not
slavishly follow the work of another. She used Crooke as she
used Du Bartas, and even Raleigh, as a reference work from
which to create her own product. In her search for useful infor-
mation to put into her poems, she wished to be as exact and
learned as possible. She turned to what was available, and she
used it in her own fashion.

Bradstreet's Humours carry on their debate in just as lively
and shrewish a fashion as did her Elements, and once again the
dramatic method gives vitality to the poem. Perhaps the best
passage is in the opening speech of Choler. Choler first claims
that she and her mother Fire were once both masculine, since
they are the noblest of the Elements and Humours, and that
they are now feminine just for a short while. Her criticism of
the Sanguine Humour is particularly witty:

> Here's sister ruddy, worth the other two,
> Who much will talk, but little dares she do,
> Unless to Court and claw, to dice and drink,
> And there she will out-bid us all, I think,
> She loves a fiddle better then a drum,
> A Chamber well, in field she dares not come,
> She'l ride a horse as bravely as the best,
> And break a staff, provided 'be in jest;
> But shuns to look on wounds, & blood that's spilt,
> She loves her sword only because its gilt.

With the sex of "sister ruddy" transposed back to masculine, the poet here is describing satirically the "character" of a Courtier or Man-about-Town. The current genre of characters will become an even stronger influence in the next of the quaternions, "The Four Ages of Man."

The second two quaternions, "The Four Ages of Man" and "The Four Seasons," were not part of the original long poem described in the letter Anne Bradstreet sent to her father in March, 1643. The later two were accompanied by a letter printed as a subscript to "The Four Seasons":

> *My Subjects bare, my Brain is bad,*
> *Or better Lines you should have had:*
> *The first fell in so nat'rally,*
> *I knew not how to pass it by;*
> *The last, though bad I could not mend.*
> *Accept therefore of what is pen'd,*
> *And all the faults that you shall spy*
> *Shall at your feet for pardon cry.*

There is no way of knowing whether "the first" which "fell in so nat'rally" was the set of two quaternions first sent to her father, or whether the poet is here referring to "The Four Ages," which is the first of this set. In either case, Anne Bradstreet's judgement of her own work was not very good from our point of view, for the last quaternion is the best of the group. In these two quaternions, and especially in the "Four Seasons," Anne Bradstreet did not have such a coherent body of material to draw upon, and she was forced to use more of her own observation and imagination.

In the "Four Elements," the poet stated her version of the ancient idea of the composition of the universe. In the "Four Humours" she used the old, but still current, theory of the composition and physiology of the little world of man. In "The Four Ages" she gives the Puritan idea of the moral nature of man, or the nature of man in relation to sin and death. "The Four Ages" contains more passages from the Bible than do all the other quaternions put together. Its theme is the vanity of man, a conscious echoing of the last two chapters of Ecclesiastes.

An introduction presents the four speakers as emblematic figures. Thus Childhood:

> Childhood was cloth'd in white & green to show
> His spring was intermixed with some snow:
> Upon his head nature a Garland set
> Of Primrose, Daizy & the Violet.
> Such cold mean flowrs the spring puts forth betime
> Before the sun hath throughly heat the clime.
> His Hobby striding did not ride but run,
> And in his hand an hour-glass new begun.

Despite the hobby horse, Childhood's monologue, in keeping with the poem's theme, is grim. He depicts none of the joys of that carefree age. Rather, his moral depravity is stressed; he is "stained from birth with *Adams* sinfull fact,/Thence I began to sin as soon as act." The more unpleasant aspects of motherhood come directly from the poet's experience. She speaks of "the nine moneths weary burthen" and the pains of childbirth. "My mother still did waste as I did thrive," says Childhood, "yet with love and all alacrity,/ Spending, was willing to be spent for me." We see the mother trying to pacify the infant:

> With wayward cryes I did disturb her rest,
> Who sought still to appease me with the breast:
> With weary arms she danc'd and *By By* sung.

When the poet describes the diseases and dangers of infancy and childhood, she has no need of books:

> What gripes of wind mine infancy did pain,
> What tortures I in breeding teeth sustain?
> What crudityes my stomack cold hath bred,
> Whence vomits, flux and worms have issued?
> What breaches, knocks and falls I daily have,
> And some perhaps I carry to my grave,
> Sometimes in fire, sometimes in water fall,
> Strangly preserv'd, yet mind it not at all:
> At home, abroad my dangers manifold,
> That wonder tis, my glass till now doth hold.

In "Childhood" the poet displays a different attitude toward love and procreation from that of the love poems. There she spoke of the wife who "long lay in thine arms," and, addressing her husband as the sun, speaks of the "fruits which through thy heat I bore." Here she speaks of the child "whose mean beginning blushing can't reveal." Nor does the poem convey the delight in children expressed later in "I had eight birds hatcht in one nest." Anne Bradstreet's attitude toward chilhood here is colored by the theme of vanity and the Puritan insistence on innate sinfulness. She was also in the midst of the trials of which she speaks; in 1643 the oldest of her then five children was no more than ten.

In drawing her portrait of mother and child, and even more in the other "Ages of Man," the poet approaches another popular genre of the time, the "character," as it appeared in such works as Bishop Hall's *The Characters of Virtues and Vices*, the translation of Theophrastus's *Characters*, the character sketches of Sir Thomas Overbury, John Earle, and others. The influence of such sketches seems particularly strong in Anne Bradstreet's portrayal of virtuous and licentious youth, and high-minded and greedy middle age. She had already described the Man-about-Town through the speech of the Sanguine Humour.

Youth bears a close resemblance to the sanguine man. His virtues are those of the good courtier and are probably modelled on those of Sir Philip Sidney, for Youth is well dressed and handsome, excellently trained in science, arts, and tongues. He knows the manners of both the court and the country and prizes "the brave attempts of valiant knights." His mirth can raise sad hearts, music enraptures his harmonious soul; though brave in the field, he is "at home to all most kind." What brings the portrait closest to Sidney, however, is the reference to battle:

> I cannot lye intrench'd before a town,
> Nor wait till good success our hopes doth crown:
> I scorn the heavy Corslet, musket-proof;
> I fly to catch the bullet thats aloof.

Sidney was with the English forces entrenched before the for-
tified town of Zutphen and was engaged in a foray against the
enemy troops when he received his death-wound. He had
thrown off part of his armor and was struck by a musket-ball.
Anne Bradstreet's whole description fits in with the almost
legendary gallantry of Sidney and could hardly fail to remind
an Englishman of her time of that hero.[24]

In coloring her general portrait of Youth with the
characteristics of a particular individual, Anne Bradstreet was
doing what some of her contemporaries had also begun to do,
that is, to merge the sketch of a type with the depiction of an
actual historical character.[25]

However, her sketch of Youth at his worst remains a picture
of a type, resembling Choler's ironic description of the
sanguine man.

> If any time from company I spare,
> 'Tis spent in curling, frisling up my hair;[26]
> Some young *Adonis* I do strive to be,
> *Sardana Pallas*, now survives in me:
> Cards, Dice, and Oaths, concomitant, I love;
> To Masques, to Playes, to Taverns stil I move;
> And in a word, if what I am you'd heare,
> Seek out a Brittish bruitish Cavaleer;
> Such wretch, such Monster am I; but yet more,
> I want a heart all this for to deplore.*

The harshness of this portrait of the Cavalier is increased if
one reads Anne Bradstreet's comments on Sardanapalus in
"The Four Monarchies." Though the Cavalier is here shown
as morally, socially, and religiously opposed to virtue, the fact
is that the Cavalier was at this time (1643 or after) also a
political opponent, and her description is doubtless politically
motivated. Satiric portrayals of the character of political and
religious groups, such as the Puritan and the Jesuit, had been
written since Elizabethan times, and the tempo of these in-
creased markedly around 1642. Anne Bradstreet in her por-
trayal of the Cavalier was undoubtedly aware of current
political writing.

In "Middle Age" she gives a sympathetic portrait of the middle-aged man:

> Yet all my powers for self ends are not spent,
> For hundreds bless me for my bounty lent.
> Whose backs I've cloth'd, and bellyes I have fed
> With mine own fleece, & with my houshold bread.

She speaks of the good done by the just magistrate, the good pastor, the skillful captain, the soldier, and the cheerful laborer, types often used by the writers of characters. Here we have a view of the characters of a small town such as Ipswich, and it will be recalled that Anne Bradstreet's husband was a justice and her brother-in-law a captain. At his worst, the middle-aged man was subject to the usual vanities. He is represented in part by the farmer who works hard, gets little rest, and finds his happiness in sordid things, such as his sheep and farrowing sow — his "dunghill thoughts" can reach no higher. This contrasts with any romantic or pastoral idealization of the farmer's life, though there will be a touch of this last in "The Four Seasons."

"Old Age" is of interest for its discussion of the political situation in England during the last years of Queen Elizabeth and subsequently. Perhaps a portrait of the poet's father,[27] in the first edition it was forthrightly favorable to the Puritan cause. The political passages were modified for the second edition to suit the changed state of affairs after the Restoration. The theme of the vanity of man's life which has run through the other Ages is stated by Old Age in greater detail. A long passage near the end of his monologue is a paraphrase of Ecclesiastes 12:1-8, to which has been added the figures of the lion and the roe from First Chronicles and the Song of Solomon. However, the poet finds an opportunity to praise another of earth's pleasures, even while discussing its vanity:

> Yea knowing much, the pleasant'st life of all,
> Hath yet among that sweet, some bitter gall.
> Though reading others Works, doth much refresh,
> Yet studying much, brings wearinesse to th' flesh.*

The strongest influences in "The Four Ages" are the Bible and the contemporary genre of characters. The introduction suggests also the influence of Spenser or of one of his followers; Anne Bradstreet has written here her only set pageant in which characters enter wearing symbolic costumes and carrying emblems. Childhood and Youth wear garlands of appropriate flowers, while Middle and Old Age carry, the one a basket of fruit, the other a sheaf of wheat. Childhood holds an hourglass just beginning to run, and Old Age bears one which is written around with the motto: *This out then am I done.*

In the next quaternion "The Four Seasons" we find other remnants of the Spenserian pastoral tradition as well as some insight into the poet's use of conventions concerned with country life and into her attitude toward nature. As in all her poetry, she does not write here a pure genre, but combines various traditions. We may identify tendencies toward pastoralism, allegory, pictorialism, and direct observation, and the poem will be considered under these headings.

Of the two forms of pastoralism to be found in Elizabethan and later poetry, one comes through the pastoral eclogue and is evidenced in Spenser's *Shepheardes Calender*. The other is an attitude toward rural life, which may, but need not, be contained in poems specifically following the formal pastoral convention. The attitude implies that country life is better because it is simpler and less vexed with cares; it is an attitude found in so many writers in the seventeenth century as to be a commonplace. Anne Bradstreet has in "Summer" a passage which is influenced by both forms. The Spenserian pastoral convention is represented in her poem by "those frolick Swains, the Shepherd Lads" who go to wash their sheep "with pipes full glad." Convention is combined with the pastoral attitude toward country life in such lines as those addressed to the shepherds:

> Blest rustick Swains, your pleasant quiet life,
> Hath envy bred in Kings that were at strife,
> Careless of worldly wealth you sing and pipe,
> Whilst they'r imbroyl'd in wars & troubles rife.

Then she refers to the shepherds envied by Bajazet, and to En-
dymion and David, classic exemplars of shepherds. The entire
passage of twenty lines derives from pastoral convention and
has little to do with a New England summer. It is for such use
of convention that Mrs. Bradstreet's work has been criticized
as bookish.[28]

Related to Spenser, too, is the presentation of the Seasons
as allegorical figures. Though there is no prologue to this
poem as there was to "The Four Ages of Man," three of the
Seasons are briefly described at the opening of their
monologues. The descriptions are not so full as in the previous
poem, and only Summer is done in any detail. She presents a
somewhat comic appearance:

> When *Spring* had done, the *Summer* did begin,
> With melted tauny face, and garments thin,
> Resembling Fire, Choler, and Middle age,
> As *Spring* did Air, Blood, Youth in's equipage.
> Wiping the sweat from off her face that ran,
> With hair all wet she puffing thus began.

Aside from such characterization, the allegorical treatment of
nature is little used, except that it is related to another techni-
que used by Anne Bradstreet and by other writers of the
Elizabethan and later period which might be called *pic-
torialism*.

By *pictorialism* I refer to a technique for describing a place
by means of a combination of realistic and unrealistic details.
The combination of realistic and unrealistic may result in
allegory, as in Spenser's Bower of Bliss, or in the unnatural
natural descriptions of Euphuism, or in the metaphoric vines
of Marvell. In each case the place is described not for the pur-
pose of natural description, but for an aesthetic effect in the
total plan of the author; description becomes a technical in-
strument rather than an end. We get only one small instance of
such pictorialism in the "Four Seasons." It is important,
however, because of criticism that Anne Bradstreet did not
describe her surroundings, but rather set down her remem-
brance of Old England. The passage to which I refer, found in
"Autumn," is a vivid catalog of the fruits of the season:

> The vintage now is ripe, the grapes are prest,
> Whose lively liquor oft is curs'd and blest:
> For nought so good, but it may be abused,
> But its a precious juice when well its used.
> The raisins now in clusters dryed be,
> The Orange, Lemon dangle on the tree:
> The Pomegranate, the Fig are ripe also,
> And apples now their yellow sides do show.
> Of Almonds,[29] Quinces, Wardens, and of Peach,
> The season's now at hand of all and each.

Bradstreet cannot here be describing a New England autumn. Oranges, lemons, pomegranates, and figs are not northern fruits; together with certain wines and raisins dried in clusters in the sun,[30] they come from the Mediterranean region. So this is not an English autumn either.[31] The passage represents autumn in the Garden of Eden, set forth for its own sake and also to support the argument that Adam was created in this season, for even in the most temperate climate, she says, this is the time when all fruits are ripe. We have seen a similar play upon conceits as argument in the love poems. In effect, the catalog of exotic fruit serves as a figure of amplification to enlarge the concept of autumn.[32]

"The Four Seasons" also includes a figure of speech that Bradstreet elaborated in the love poems, the Sun-earth, Lover-beloved metaphor. It appears most notably in "Spring":

> The Primrose pale, and azure violet
> Among the virduous grass hath nature set,
> That when the Sun on's Love (the earth) doth shine
> These might as lace set out her garment fine.
> . . . .
> The Sun now enters loving *Gemini*,
> And heats us with the glances of his eye,
> Our thicker rayment makes us lay aside
> Lest by his fervor we be torrifi'd.

We feel here once more the same sensuality of imagery that appeared in the love poems — the beloved preening herself to receive the amorous glances of the lover, who brings about

love and procreation through his heat. In "Autumn" the poet
adds another dimension to the sun metaphor for she makes the
Sun represent the Redeemer:

So doth old Age still tend unto his grave,
Where also he his winter time must have;
But when the Sun of righteousness draws nigh,
His dead old stock, shall mount again on high.

Thus to the image of the relationship of Sun-earth, Lover-
beloved, she brings that of Redeemer-redeemed. And we shall
see later in her last farewell to the world the Redeemer greeted
as the loving bridegroom.

But Anne Bradstreet meant to do more in "The Four
Seasons" than introduce allegorical figures and ingenious
metaphors. Her central purpose, as in the other quaternions,
was to present some sort of knowledge, either practical or
moral. The "useful" knowledge here mostly concerns
astronomy and the zodiac. Beginning with the month of
March, the first month of the year according to the old calen-
dar, Anne Bradstreet mentions the heavenly sign as each
month is introduced. She also notes the equinoxes and the
longest and shortest days. There is little moralizing beyond
that usually involved in the pastoral convention and the com-
ment that the yellow leaves of autumn signify that age must
also have its time.

The major portion of the poem is taken up with an almost
lyric celebration of the seasons in New England and a descrip-
tion of the activities that belong to each. Among those she
mentions are the pursuits of the plowman, the seeds-man, and
the gardener, who erects poles for his hops and manures and
trims his trees. It is spring, and the frogs come chirping out
and "hop about the field." The birds nest, the clucking hen
leads out her chicks. The orchards bloom. The housewife in
her dairy fills her shelves for winter time. In summer, it is hot
as an oven after the coals have been withdrawn. The housewife
distills rosewater. Cherries, gooseberries, and peas are in their
prime. The mowers go to the meadows, the reapers to the
wheat fields. And the late fruits ripen. Autumn is a time for

solid meats, warm clothes, good fires. But Bradstreet has little
to say for winter. Obviously she does not like this season. The
section on winter is the shortest, and she inserts a line in which
she gives her own opinion, rather than that of the character
who is speaking: "I care not how the winter time doth haste."

The Duyckincks in their *Cyclopaedia of American
Literature* objected to her lack of taste in her literal references
to the shepherds rubbing the dirty fleeces of the sheep in the
stream, and to the line "And solid'st meats our stomachs can
digest."*[33] Morison on the other hand, criticizes those
historians of American literature who condescend to her as
merely imitative and as merely describing English scenery.
Using "Contemplations" as an example, he contends that
New England furnished the material of her later poetry.[34] An
examination of the description contained in the "Four
Seasons" indicates that this is true of her earlier work as well,
though of course the New England rural activities are modell-
ed on those of England. The fact that she used English names
for birds and flowers does not necessarily mean that she was
not looking at the American landscape. Her poem called for
concrete terms, and she used ones she knew. Anne Bradstreet
continually described what was around her in the realms both
of ideas and of physical landscape. Over and over she used
what she saw to fill out the conventions she encountered in her
reading.

Hence her shepherds do not act entirely like the idyllic
creatures of convention. Though they sing and play on pipes,
their sheep get dirty and need to be washed. In the same way,
the emblematic figure of Childhood, with his hobby-horse and
hourglass, precedes a description of real children who get
worms and stomach-aches. We find further evidence of her
movement toward realism in comparing her Seasons with the
procession of Seasons and Months in Spenser's "Cantos of
Mutability." Her treatment contains enough similarities to
suggest she was familiar with that work, but in Bradstreet's
"Fall" and "Winter" the cold comes down earlier and harder
than in Spenser's Ireland. For her, September rather than Oc-
tober is the month for wine-making. For her, warm fires are

called for by November rather than December; timber is felled in November, too, rather than January. And while Spenser's January woodcutter blows on his nails to keep warm, in Bradstreet's New England December "Toes and Ears, and Fingers often freeze,/And Travellers their noses sometimes leese."

In keeping with the Bradstreet penchant for humor, the allegorical figure of Summer, which in Spenser remains dignified despite the sweat that drips from under his garland, resembles in Bradstreet a blowzy New England goodwife puffing from exertion and wiping sweat off her face. She takes her place beside other comic characters of early American humor — the gentlewomen turned out as "gant bar-geese" in Ward's *Simple Cobbler* and, later, Irving's brawny Minerva tucking up her skirts outside Fort Christina.

But for the most part "The Four Ages" and "The Four Seasons" lack the sarcastic wit of the first two quaternions. "The Four Ages" is grim, more concerned with life's vexations than its triumphs. "The Four Seasons" has qualities of serious lyric that will be developed later in "Contemplations." The characters in these quaternions do not quarrel among themselves — in fact, they ignore one another. Their successive monologues resemble those of a masque or pageant. They are, in fact, a Spenserian procession transplanted from Elizabethan England to the the realism of Anne Bradstreet's New England. In them the dispute among the characters that occupied the first two quaternions continues within the poet herself. Particularly in "The Four Ages," she begins an argument running counter to her love of this world and its goods — that of the vanity of this world — a theme that will become stronger in her later work. But an additional theme emerges also, a growing interest in the world of nature, for in the last of the quaternions, the New England landscape has become the landscape of home.

Emblematic figure from Francis Quarles' *Emblemes*, 1635, showing Folly in the guise of a child.

CHAPTER 4
A DIALOGUE BETWEEN OLD ENGLAND AND NEW

Anne Bradstreet's acceptance of New England as a homeland is further demonstrated in her next poem. This time she takes as her subject another worldly dispute, from yet a different arena, that of politics. She shows herself keenly aware of the growing crisis between the King and the Puritan party in England. And at every stage of the crisis she demonstrates the point of view of one who has adopted New England as a now-and-future home. Once more she uses personification in dialogue, and again she turns to a popular genre for her model, this time one used by both Puritan and Cavalier for describing current events.

She was no doubt acquainted with at least some of the broadsides that after the year 1639 poured from the presses — a sometimes clandestine but always popular means of distributing news about the war, including comments on its leading figures. Despite Puritan censure of the love stories or the tales of gruesome crimes they often contained, writers on both sides of the civil dispute engaged in the production of broadsides, often in the form of poems, especially ballads. Anne Bradstreet's "Dialogue between Old England and New" is longer and more scholarly than most of the broadside ballads, as befits a spectator far from the scene of action who has time to reflect upon events. But her poem retains many of their features, notably the recital of recent events and the hard-hitting, sometimes crude, often satiric, comment. Other characteristics of some, though not all, of the broadsides were the dialogue form and the concluding exhortation, which directed the reader or the characters in the ballad to undertake certain actions, just as does the modern political speech or pamphlet. The "Dialogue" may even be thought of as one of the early pieces of editorial journalism in New England, for no doubt it circulated in manuscript among the people of Ipswich

and perhaps that of other towns as well. For her readers in
New England, it summed up their reactions to what was then
occurring as well as their remembrance of the causes that led
to "the present troubles."

As those on the side of Parliament clearly saw, and as Old
England and her daughter New England relate, the roots of
the current crisis lay deep in history. The two characters cite
disturbances in England all the way back to the invasions of
the Saxons and Danes.[1] But the history of most importance to
New Englanders concerned the more recent emigration of the
Saints and the state of mind in which they undertood their
planting of the New Canaan. Old England describes the suf-
ferings of the preachers and prophets among the Puritans and
recalls that her pulpits had rung with denunciations of sin and
the imminent and terrible punishment of God. She recounts
the nation's "sins, the breach of sacred Lawes," and cites the
warnings given by the Protestant troubles in Germany and in
France and the atrocities reported from Ireland. She refers,
punningly, to the Root and Branch Petition presented to the
House of Commons, December 11, 1640, which attempted to
abolish the episcopacy, and the committing of Archbishop
Laud to the Tower, which took place in February, 1641. In one
of her most savage lines she remarks on the beheading of
Strafford in May, saying, "They took high Strafford lower by
the head." She refers also to the introduction on December 7,
1641, of the Militia Bill, which would place all military and
naval appointments under the direct control of Parliament.
The Militia Bill was an important subject of dispute between
Charles and Parliament in the first months of 1642. On March
15, 1642, the king acquainted the houses of Parliament with
his intention to reside at York. Anne Bradstreet reports:

> The King displeas'd at *York* himself absents,
> They humbly beg return, shew their intents;
> The writing, printing, posting too and fro,
> Shews all was done, I'le therefore let it go.

The words of a Parliament man regarding this period are
strikingly similar: "Beacons are new made, sea-marks set up,

and great posting up and down with packets; all symptoms of ensuing war."[2] Anne Bradstreet also urges on the Earl of Essex, who was appointed general of the Parliamentary forces early in July, with the words, "Go on brave *Essex.*"

Earlier in the year, on February 23, a fast day had been observed in London for the sins of the nation. Stephen Marshall preached at Westminster from the text in Judges 5:23: "Curse ye Meroz, said the angel of the Lord, curse ye bitterly the inhabitants thereof; because they came not to the help of the Lord, to the help of the Lord against the mighty."[3] Marshall had preached the sermon two months before at St. Sepulchre's; its popularity was so great that he is reported to have ultimately delivered it threescore times. Edmund Hickeringill, writing in 1680, refers to the Meroz theme as having "usher'd in, as well as promoted, the late bloody civil wars." The sermon came out in at least four editions by the end of 1642, and Anne Bradstreet picked up its theme in the "Dialogue":

> Blest be thy Preachers, who do chear thee on,
> O cry the Sword of God, and *Gideon:*
> And shall I not on them wish *Mero's* curse,
> That help thee not with prayers, Arms, and purse?

The entire poem indicates that the news from England was received with interest and set down analytically by the poet as a current extension of history. If the contention wherein

> They worded it so long, they fell to blows,
> That thousands lay on heaps, here bleeds my woes,
> I that no wars so many years have known,
> Am now destroy'd and slaught'red by mine own

refers to the opening battles of the Civil War which began with Edgehill in late October of 1642, the latest reports from England were receiving prompt use at the hands of the poet.

As Puritans and as members of a society many of whose members had been oppressed by the Laudian regime, the magistrates and people of Massachusetts Bay were generally

on the side of Parliament. Bradstreet makes this explicit in her
concluding lines in the first edition:

> Farewell dear mother, Parliament, prevail,
> And in a while you'l tell another tale.*

As an ardent partisan, Bradstreet despises the Cavalier. The
Cavalier is not mentioned in this poem, but as we have seen in
"Youth" he is shown in the blackest of colors. Her dark view
may have been deepened by the stories of atrocities coming
from Ireland, and the identity which some Englishmen found
between Irish rebel and English royalist. "An Irish Rebel and
an English Cavallier," Hugh Peter commented after his return
from Ireland, "in words and actions we found as unlike as an
egge is to an egge."[4] Anne Bradstreet's own version of the
Irish rebellion was mentioned by *Old Age* in the first edition,
but was expanded in the second:

> I've seen and so have you, for tis but late,
> The desolation of goodly State,
> Plotted and acted so that none can tell,
> Who gave the counsel, but the Prince of hell,
> Three hundred thousand slaughtered innocents,
> By bloudy Popish, hellish miscreants:
> Oh may you live, and so you will I trust
> To see them swill in bloud untill they burst.

The vengefulness added by the poet when she revised came
after a reading of Sir John Temple's *History of the Irish
Rebellion*, published in 1646. Temple, who was Master of the
Rolls in Dublin in 1641, gives a horrifying and detailed ac-
count of the persecution of the Irish Protestants.[5]

With the extension of the troubles in Scotland and Ireland
to England, it became obvious that if the Bay Colony were to
serve as an example to all the Protestant world, the time
should be at hand. If New England were to serve in the armies
of the Lord, the time had come. But neither of these purposes
was she able to fulfill.

Anne Bradstreet expresses the inability of New England to
support Parliament by money or men: "Your humble Child

intreats you, shew your grief,/ Though Arms, nor Purse she hath for your relief,/ Such is her poverty."

What could New England do? She could pray. William Hooke, minister at Taunton, called for such spiritual aid as early as July 23, 1640, a day of public humiliation appointed by the churches in behalf of their native country. His sermon, called *New Englands Teares, For Old Englands Feares*, reflected on the imminent danger of a clash between the two "sister nations" of England and Scotland in the Second Bishop's War. Hooke's sermon was published in London in 1641 and no doubt copies found their way back to the Bay. Probably Anne Bradstreet had one, for the sermon contains a number of ideas and phrases that occur in her "Dialogue."[6] Hooke expresses the closeness of the two "nations" by stating that some of the punishment now being inflicted on Old England is the result of the sins of those who left for New England, and goes on to describe in detail how the misdeeds they committed there had bred still more sin in the people who remained in England. Anne Bradstreet also expresses the responsibility in the person of *New-England*:

> Your fearfull sins great cause there's to lament,
> My guilty hands in part, hold up with you,
> A Sharer in your punishment's my due.

Though New England has shared in the sins of Old England, she can help by her prayers to turn away the Lord's wrath. There is even a slight indication that the prayers of New England may be more efficacious than those of *Old England*, though the effect of the lines may be simply the result of the metaphoric structure. *Old England* says:

> This Physick purging potion, I have taken,
> Will bring consumption, or an Ague quaking,
> Unless some Cordial, thou fetch from high,
> Which present help may ease my malady.

The point about the special appeal that *New England* may make to the deity is reinforced when *Old England* says:

> Famine, and Plague, two sisters of the Sword,
> Destruction to a Land doth soone afford;
> They're for my punishments ordain'd on high,
> Unless thy teares prevent it speedily.*

Besides bringing the gift of supplication for which she has a special talent, New England has yet another way to help the mother country. She can sympathize. The element of sympathy, implicit in the title of Hooke's sermon *New Englands Teares, for Old Englands Feares,* is stressed throughout the sermon itself: "It is a great lightning of the afflictions of brethren, to be bemoaned by brethren and friends in time of affliction... But the use that I doe principally intend, is of Exhortation to you all, as you desire to approve your selves the true friends and brethren of your deare Countrey-men in old *England*, to condole with them... in their afflictions." Anne Bradstreet, too, rings in the note of sympathy in *New-England's* opening speech, which asks about *Old England's* woes, and ends, "Ah, tell thy daughter, she may sympathize." Later *New-England* states:

> Pray in plain termes, what is your present grief,
> Then let's join heads, and hands for your relief.*

Although the failure of the "errand into the wilderness" was not to be fully reckoned with until the 1660's when the colonists and their preachers felt the force of "God's controversy with New England," the failure itself occurred in the 1640's when the reformed churches of England did not take the New England churches as their model. England did not accept the New England way, and the New England Puritans were criticized for having left the scene of turmoil.

The alienation is seen in works like Hooke's sermon and Anne Bradstreet's dialogue, though their purpose is to state the solidarity of the two Englands, and though Marshall had specifically asked for sympathy, tears and prayers. Hooke preached his sermon two years before the Civil War had actually begun. He tried to persuade his hearers to disallow war by a graphic description of its miseries, the slaughter of young men, the weeping of widows and orphans, fires, famines, pestilence, murder, the "ravishing of matrones, deflouring of virgins," and other cruelties. But when Bradstreet wrote, the die was already cast. In the character of Old England, she passes over war's horrors rather quickly, though using terms perhaps suggested by Hooke: "My plundered Townes, my houses devastation,/ My ravisht virgins, and my young men slain,/ My wealthy trading faln, my dearth of grain,/ The seed time's come, but Ploughman hath no hope,/ Because he knows not, who shall inn his crop:/ The poore they want their pay, their children bread,/ Their wofull mother's tears unpitied."* And in a dispassionate manner, possible for one so far from the scene of danger, New England consoles her mother by listing the aims of the war:

> Your griefs I pity much, but should do wrong,
> To weep for that we both have pray'd for long,
> To see these latter dayes of hop'd for good,
> That Right may have its right, though't be with blood;
>
> . . . .
>
> These are the dayes, the Churches foes to crush,
> To root out Prelates, head, tail, branch, and rush.[7]
> Let's bring *Baals* vestments out, to make a fire,
> Their Myters, Surplices, and all their tire,
> Copes, Rochets, Crossiers, and such trash.*

She then describes the halcyon days that will come about after those who hurt Charles' people and his Crown are destroyed. Under Charles, the church and commonweal will be reestablished in a proper manner, and the prerogative courts will be done away with. In 1642 Anne Bradstreet still clung to the notion that Charles was the victim of evil counselors and might be redeemed from them. The Parliamentary army is really on the side of the King.

Her vision goes beyond the end of the Civil War and penetrates into the millennium to come. In the seventeenth century the obscure vision of the four beasts in the book of Daniel was thought to represent the four great empires that Anne Bradstreet would later write about in "The Four

Monarchies." The little horn that appeared on the head of the
fourth beast and which warred on the Saints was symbolic of
the papacy. During the civil war, many believed that the forces
opposing the king were fighting the battles of Christ and mak-
ing way for his kingdom. The events of the Thirty Years' War
on the continent had encouraged the idea that the Roman em-
pire was about to end, and that the fifth monarchy with Christ
as its king would soon come into being. In the coming of the
kingdom, the Jews were to be converted, and the
Mohammedans, other heathens, and Papists would be over-
come. Christ himself would appear. Just when was not certain,
and the order of events differed in the various
prognostications.

The idea of the imminence of the millennium was widely
held in America. John Cotton, in the early part of 1640,
preached a series of sermons on the beasts in the thirteenth
chapter of Revelation, in which he spoke of the first three
beasts of Daniel as the monarchs of Babel, Persia, and Greece.
He identified the first beast of Revelations 13 as the Roman
Catholic visible church and commented that, as demonstrated
in the past, no wars against the Turks would prosper until the
papacy was overthrown.[8]

Anne Bradstreet, identifying the Papcy as "the Beast that
rul'd the World," calls for a crusade by Old England against
Rome. Once Englishmen have conquered that "filthy den,"
she urges them to go on to Turkey and lay it waste in fulfill-
ment of "the sacred doom." That done, she confidently
predicts the conversion of "Abraham's seed" and the coming
of days of "happiness and rest."

A formal seventeenth-century sermon usually ended with a
section of *Uses* in which doctrine was translated into a
program of action. New England's long last speech outlines
such a program. Moreover, New England calls down blessings
on the various political estates — nobles, commons, and coun-
ties — along with the army and the preachers who cheer it on.
In dispensing blessings and exhorting the whole nation to ac-
tion, New England sounds like a preacher herself. Writing
without the mask of a persona, Anne Bradstreet, who so often

apologized at the beginning or ending of her poems, could not have been so bold. Indeed, this is the only time she used the exhortation anywhere. But her vigorous use of the imperative in "The Dialogue" came also because she took as her cues to form and content two of the most public forms of early seventeenth-century writing — the broadside ballad and the sermon. Following such models she came close to assuming two roles generally forbidden to women — those of the broadside balladeer or journalist and the preacher.[9]

Frontispiece from Sir Walter Raleigh's *History of the World*, 1614, with allegorical figures.

CHAPTER 5
THE PROLOGUE AND THE FOUR MONARCHIES

The years 1641-1643 found Anne Bradstreet at the peak of the period of her early, public poetry. During those years she produced the elegies on Du Bartas and Elizabeth, the first two quaternions, the "Dialogue between Old England and New" and probably the poetic letters to her husband as well. She may also have finished the second two quaternions during 1643, and possibly part of the "Four Monarchies." This is a large production for any poet, let alone one who snatched her time for writing "from sleep and other refreshments." The poems demonstrate an increasing variety of techniques, subjects, and genres, and an increasing confidence in and mastery of her art. Surely she had more than fulfilled the promise she made in the Du Bartas elegy of 1641 to make further offerings of verse.

Sometime, however, after she had written enough poems to have her reputation as a poet bruited about the settlement — and this may have been around 1642-1643 — the poet ran into the snag of prejudice against her sex. She had inherited enough of her father's stubbornness to defy, rather than cringe at, criticism. Her reply to critics took the form — again — of poetry. "The Prologue" is both an apology for her poetry and a defense of her right to compose; in defending herself, she defended other women as well.

An apology for lack of skill was a device present in much poetry of the time. Spenser employed it in his eclogues and in *Astrophel*; Sylvester devoted many lines to it. A statement of the author's lack of art occurred frequently in the New England funeral elegy. In the Sidney and Du Bartas elegies Anne Bradstreet apologizes by describing the problems that beset her and her muse, and she comments on her lack of skill

63

here and there in other poems. In the elegy on Elizabeth
"Mongst hundred Hecatombs of roaring Verse," hers
"bleating stands" before the royal hearse. In verse letters she
tells her father that the first two quaternions are "rudely pen'd"
by her "humble hand"; her rhymes are "harsh," her lines
"ragged," and after the second two quaternions, she com-
plains: "My Subjects bare, my Brain is bad."

"The Prologue" is not an apology like these others,
however, but a defense of herself as a woman who dared to
write. Probably by this time her writing had come to the atten-
tion of Governor Winthrop himself. His daughter Mary was
married to Anne's brother Samuel Dudley, and the couple liv-
ed for a while in Ipswich. Doubtless Mary Dudley saw the
poems that were so proudly displayed among Anne's relatives,
and perhaps she sent some of them to the governor. The
forthright governor may have expressed himself to Anne or
her family on the subject of women's place in terms similar to
those he used in the often quoted journal entry of April 13,
1645, to describe Anne Hopkins, "who was fallen into a sad
infirmity, the loss of her understanding and reason, which had
been growing upon her divers years, by occasion of her giving
herself wholly to reading and writing, and had written many
books. Her husband, being very loving and tender of her, was
loath to grieve her; but he saw his errour, when it was too late.
For if she had attended her household affairs, and such things
as belong to women, and not gone out of her way and calling
to meddle in such things as are proper for men, whose minds
are stronger &c. she had kept her wits, and might have im-
proved them usefully and honourably in the place God had set
her."[1]

From whatever source the criticism came, Mistress
Bradstreet smarted under it but did not give in. "The
Prologue" opens with an echo of Virgil's line "Arms and the
man I sing" which begins the Aeneid. She denies that she will
strive for such poetic heights: "To sing of Wars, of Captains,
and of Kings,/ Of Cities founded, Common-wealths begun,/
For my mean pen, are too superiour things." The denial seems
strange, inasmuch as she had just written — or would soon

write — her "Dialogue between Old England and New" and her "Four Monarchies," the subject of both being certainly wars, captains, and kings, and their exploits; indeed in her whole canon, images of war and royalty far outnumber household images. She goes on for four stanzas apologizing for her "blemished Muse." But in the last four stanzas, she defies her critics, not without a conciliatory bow to the preeminence of men. "The Prologue" is a witty defense, giving in on enough points to make the main thrust of her argument seem reasonable. And she ends with the usual indication that she will continue to write and now even hopes to achieve some sort of recognition in the form of a parsley wreath.[2]

The criticism which Anne Bradstreet encountered during this period may have caused her to continue her defense of women with the elegy on Queen Elizabeth, written in 1643. Queen Elizabeth represented not only a pattern of royalty against which to measure the Stuart kings, but her virtues comprised the best argument to refute the critics of women. Bradstreet, after the introductory poem, gets directly to this point: "She hath wip'd off th' aspersion of her Sex,/ That women wisdome lack to play the Rex." Toward the end of the elegy, she turns again to the theme of women's ability:

> Now say, have women worth? or have they none?
> Or had they some, but with our Queen ist gone?
> Nay Masculines, you have thus tax'd us long,
> But she though dead, will vindicate our wrong.
> Let such, as say our sex is void of reason,
> Know 'tis a slander now, but once was treason.*

In this passage she departs from her tribute in order to use the Queen as an argument in favor of intelligence of women and against the "carping tongues" of her own detractors.

Having delivered herself of her spirited defenses of women's ability to think and to write, Anne Bradstreet turned to an even more ambitious project than she had yet undertaken — a long, dull, and for the modern reader, exasperating, project that would occupy her for many years to come.[3]

Even had she been ignorant of John Cotton's sermon on the four beasts in Daniel, Anne Bradstreet might have turned naturally to the subject of "The Four Monarchies" as a logical sequel to her series of fours. She had already demonstrated her knowledge of history in "Old Age," in the elegies on Du Bartas and Elizabeth, and in the "Dialogue between Old England and New." In "Old Age" she called "knowing much" the "pleasant'st life of all." The knowledge to be gained through history was valuable both to those who could use its lessons in guiding the state and to private persons who could see divine justice being worked out over generations of men. Richard Norton, whose translation of Camden Anne Bradstreet used, had written "great is the pleasure of reading Histories; so naturall unto man is the desire of knowledge," and Puttenham had gone even further to claim that "the Poesie historical is of all other next the divine most honorable and worthy, as well for the common benefit as for the speciall comfort every man receiveth by it." Books of history vied with sermons to form the bulk of Puritan libraries. Anne Bradstreet's father owned Grimstone's *Generall Historie of the Netherlands,* Knolles' *Generall Historie of the Turkes,* Tymme's *Commentaries... of the Civill Warres of France,* Camden's *Annales Rerum Anglicarum et Hibernicarum regnante Elizabetha*, and Buchanan's *Rerum Scoticarum historia*, in addition to Holland's translation of Livy's *History of Rome*.[4] The poet herself referred to Plutarch, Sir Walter Raleigh, Archbishop James Usher, William Pemble, John Speed, William Camden, and Richard Knolles, historians whose works were either written in, or translated into, English. To a person not particularly excited by the fine points of religious doctrine, the histories must have been among the most interesting reading available in the colony.

Though her reading in history was broad, Anne Bradstreet based her "Four Monarchies" almost entirely on Sir Walter Raleigh's *History of the World*.[5] However, she did not follow him in beginning with the histories of Palestine and Egypt. She confined her poems to the four kingdoms which since early Christian times were supposed to be foreshadowed in the Book of Daniel (Ch. 7) — the Assyrian, Persian, Grecian, and Roman empires. She was particularly interested in the rise and fall of these empires because she believed that the time for the overthrow of the fourth monarchy (the papacy) was at hand, as she states in the conclusion of her "Old England and New."

Her rewriting of Raleigh reflects a broadening of the method she used in that poem, where she explained the present in terms of the past. The emigration to the New World was part of the large divine plan begun in Biblical times and nearing its climax in contemporary events. In her exposure of the roots of the present, Anne Bradstreet took the Puritan mission in America as seriously as did other Puritan chroniclers of contemporary events.

Her aim in demonstrating the working out of the vision of Daniel explains her treatment of the four monarchies as separate and successive in time. This is a change from Raleigh, who considers together events that occurred at the same time, though in different kingdoms. Anne Bradstreet excludes all that does not contribute to the picture of a series of kings, their characters, deeds, and succession. She further simplifies her history by omitting the long discussions of disputed points to be found in Raleigh. She chooses from his book the version which appears most likely, sometimes with a mention of the dispute, but it does not serve her purpose to become involved in argument. In the details she selects, however, she closely approximates Raleigh's words and the order of his narration, as may be seen by comparing any part of her text with her source.

Following the theory of Raleigh as he outlines it in his "Introduction" Anne Bradstreet shows history working out the pattern of divine justice in the shorter range of several generations. In Book IV, especially, Raleigh does this again and again in describing the wars that broke out between Alexander's commanders after the conqueror's death, the supreme example of divine retribution being the complete destruction of Alexander's line. Anne Bradstreet, likewise, shows the execution of divine justice, saying, "Now blood was paid with blood for what was done/ By cruel Father, Mother, cruel

Son." The over-arching purpose of showing the long past as part of the divine pattern required that the past be accurately depicted. Hence, time and time again Anne Bradstreet tells a legend or gives the reported size of an army, with such comments as: these tales "are fit for such, whose ears for Fables itch," or "but that I doubt." Much of this skepticism is also found in Raleigh. In preparation for the second edition, the author changed her poem to accord with other sources. For example, Raleigh identifies Ninias, the Assyrian king, with Amraphel, who lived about the same time as Abram; Bradstreet, in the second edition, adds a dozen lines to say that Archbishop Usher comes nearer the truth in assigning Ninias a much later date. Archbishop Usher's *Annals of the World* was published in 1658 after the first version of the "Four Monarchies" had appeared. Some of the figures she uses for the lengths of reigns of kings also come from a source other than Raleigh.

But despite her care for accuracy of detail, Anne Bradstreet was not able to describe the conflicts of the last part of the Grecian monarchy with any clarity. In the first two monarchies, she had managed fairly well by assembling Raleigh's material under the name of each king, giving a list of his accomplishments and weaknesses. But so simple a structure could not adequately render Raleigh's elaborate account of the wars among the Greeks over the spoils of Alexander's empire. The poet realized this by the time she reached the conclusion of the Grecian monarchy. She included an apology for undertaking so high a subject, and contradicted the self-assertion of "The Prologue" by declaring that "This task befits not women like to men."

Her real problem in "The Four Monarchies," however, was not her sex, but that rhymed historical description did not allow a display of her own true genius. Almost all her other poetry becomes viable through some sort of argument — the forthright satiric comments of the first quaternions, the lyric contrasts among the seasons, the argument in the later poems between the visible and invisible. In most of her poems, Bradstreet makes the presence of a character, or her own

personal voice, felt; there is a narrator, an "I," within the
poem. But, except in one short passage, the poet does not enter
"The Four Monarchies." The poem is straight third-person
narration, which, moving swiftly as it does from one character
to another over the centuries, never focusses on one situation
long enough for the poet to gain the reader's ongoing
attention. Not realizing that her problem lay in the very
structure of her history, the weary poet did not give over her
task at the end of the Grecian Monarchy. After reconsidering,
she spoke once more with all the gusto of a writer who has
become totally involved in a subject:

> After some dayes of rest, my restless heart
> To finish what's begun, new thoughts impart,
> And maugre all resolves, my fancy wrought
> This fourth to th' other three, now might be brought.

The fourth monarchy was not destined to be finished.
Raleigh's treatment of the Roman empire is lengthy; as the
poet said, "The subject large my mind and body weak" — and
her fancy was not strong enough to carry the burden beyond
106 lines — the end of the period of the Roman kings — at
least during her early period.

In "An Apology" placed at the end of the "Roman
Monarchy" in the second edition she tells how, long
afterward, she renewed the attempt to carry on the poem
presumably to the present rule of the Pope:

> At length resolv'd, when many years had past,
> To prosecute my story to the last;
> And for the same, I hours not few did spend,
> And weary lines (though lanke) I many pen'd:
> But 'fore I could accomplish my desire,
> My papers fell a prey to th' raging fire.

The fire was that which destroyed the Bradstreet house in An-
dover in 1666, and which may have destroyed other of Anne
Bradstreet's poems as well as the fourth kingdom.

Despite the author's misgivings about her "lank" lines,
however, and the modern view of the poem as a failure, "The

Four Monarchies" probably helped the development of its author as a poet. Apparently her friends and family liked the poem. Her publisher thought enough of it to make "The Four Monarchies" an important part of the subtitle of her book, perhaps hoping to capitalize on the millenarian interest of the 1650's. Her poem made available in a simple and direct form material hidden in over four of Raleigh's heavy five volumes. And Anne Bradstreet herself was satisfied enough with the reception of the portion she had written to try later to complete the work.

Finally, as she searched with Raleigh through history for the workings of the divine plan made manifest, she found evidence to bolster her faith in the invisible — a faith in which she often wavered. Her long involvement with the ashes of the past adds the solidity of knowledge to later passages on the transitoriness of even the greatest of mortal things.

CHAPTER 6
THE TENTH MUSE

While the poet's interest in history as continuum was leading her from the most recent news all the way back to the remote kingdoms of the past, the political crisis in England was working to break up the Ipswich circle. With the overthrow of the Laudian regime and the outbreak of civil war, England needed the services of her self-exiled citizens, and the tide of emigration turned once more toward, rather than away from, the homeland.

In the winter of 1646-47 Nathaniel Ward returned to England, and on a fast day, June 30, 1647, he preached before the House of Commons on the text of Ezekiel 19:14. The sermon was entered in the *Stationers Register* on July 7, 1647, by Stephen Bowtell at the sign of the Bible in Popes Head-Alley. Much of Bowtell's publishing consisted of sermons; the bulk of his entries in the *Register*, at least prior to 1650, are of sermons delivered before one or both houses of Parliament by Stephen Marshall, the author of *Meroz Curse*. Later in 1647 Bowtell also published Ward's book *The Simple Cobler of Aggawam in America*.

In 1647 Giles Firmin, the physician of Ipswich and Ward's son-in-law, left for England, and in the same year Anne Bradstreet's brother-in-law John Woodbridge went there at "the invitation of his friends."[1] His younger brother Benjamin Woodbridge had already returned shortly after his graduation from Harvard in 1642.

But though so many of Anne Bradstreet's friends were gone to the Old England, they did not forget the poet in the New. Someone, perhaps Anne's sister Mercy, the wife of John Woodbridge, or perhaps Woodbridge himself, or possibly Nathaniel Ward, took copies of Anne Bradstreet's poems back to England. There they must have circulated in manuscript, for her editor says: ". . .I found that diverse had

71

gotten some scattered Papers, affected them well, were likely to have sent forth broken pieces, to the Authors prejudice."

It was Anne Bradstreet's brother-in-law John Woodbridge who decided to allow the poems to be published all together, rather than be seen as "broken pieces." The publishing was undertaken once more by Stephen Bowtell, who, on July 1, 1650, had entered in the *Stationers Register* "a booke called The tenth muse lately sprung up in America, written by Ann Bradstreet."

There was no time to send to America for the author's consent to publish or for a corrected manuscript. John Woodbridge wrote in his poem:

'Tis true, it doth not now so neatly stand,
As if 'twere pollisht with your own sweet hand;
'Tis not so richly deckt, so trimly tir'd,
Yet it is such as justly is admir'd.

The book appeared later the same year under the lengthy title: "THE TENTH MUSE Lately sprung up in AMERICA. OR Severall Poems, compiled with great variety of Wit and Learning, full of delight. Wherein especially is contained a compleat discourse and description of the Four *Elements, Constitutions, Ages of Man, Seasons of the Year.* Together with an Exact Epitomie of the Four Monarchies,*viz.* The *Assyrian, Persian, Grecian, Roman.* Also a Dialogue between Old *England* and New, concerning the late troubles. With divers other pleasant and serious Poems. By a Gentlewoman in those parts." For all its long title it was a dainty little book, a sextodecimo of xiv and 207 pages.

John Woodbridge wrote the foreword and following it were a number of commendatory poems, including one by Nathaniel Ward. Ward good-naturedly compared Bradstreet's book to that of Du Bartas; others called her a star, one of the Muses, or the moon which has eclipsed the sun. The New England poet, whose muse so ardently wished for fame, had at last achieved the permanence of print.

Yet John Woodbridge said in the foreword that in publishing the book he feared the displeasure of no one but the author. As he predicted, when Anne Bradstreet received a copy, her reaction was not immediately one of pleasure. She was indeed embarrassed. Woodbridge had likened her book to a child; addressing his poem to his "sister" he said:

> If't be a fault, 'tis mine, 'tis shame that might
> Deny so fair an Infant of its right
> To look abroad; I know your modest mind,
> How you will blush, complain, 'tis too unkind:
> To force a womans birth, provoke her pain,
> Expose her labours to the Worlds disdain.

Catching up the image of the child, Anne Bradstreet replied in a poem addressed to her book, calling it "Thou ill-form'd offspring of my feeble brain." Her little poem ends on a note similar to that of Spenser in the lines "To His Booke" at the beginning of *The Shepheardes Calender*. She says:

> If for thy Father askt, say, thou hadst none:
> And for thy Mother, she alas is poor,
> Which caus'd her thus to send thee out of door.

Spenser, too, uses the metaphor of the child, saying, "thy selfe present,/ As child whose parent is unkent." He inquires after the parent of the book in the lines "And asked, who thee forth did bring" and "But if that any aske thy name,/ Say thou wert base begot with blame." The similarity reinforces the possibility that Bradstreet was familiar with *The Shepheardes Calender*.

After her initial reactions to the flaws, the poet began to feel the pride natural to an author who first sees her work in print and began to revise the poems:

> Yet being mine own, at length affection would
> Thy blemishes amend, if so I could:
> I wash'd thy face, but more defects I saw,
> And rubbing off a spot, still made a flaw.
> I stretcht thy joynts to make thee even feet,
> Yet still thou run'st more hobling then is meet;
> In better dress to trim thee was my mind,
> But nought save home-spun Cloth, i'th' house I find.

A comparison between the first edition of her book and the second "corrected by the Author," shows the extensive changes made in order to attain "even feet," and to "trim" the book "in better dress." The changes amount most frequently to the substitution of one similar word for another, though in some of the poems, notably in the Sidney elegy, the "Dialogue between Old England and New" and the "Four Monarchies," there are deletions and substitutions of entire passages.

Despite the author's, misgivings, *The Tenth Muse* was attractive enough to readers that eight years later in 1658, William London listed "The 10. Muse, a Poem" by Mrs. Bradstreet in his *Catalogue of the Most Vendible Books in England*. In 1673 Bathsua Makin, an educated Englishwoman who had been tutor to the daughters of Charles I and had kept schools for the daughters of the nobility, in *An Essay to Revive the Ancient Education of Gentlewomen in Religion, Manners, Arts & Tongues* praised the work of Anne Bradstreet.[2] And in 1675, twenty-five years after the publication of *The Tenth Muse*, Edward Phillips in his *Theatrum Poetarum* said that the memory of her *Tenth Muse* was "not yet totally extinct." A book by Anne Bradstreet was the only volume of English poetry listed in the library of Edward Taylor at the time of his death, and later in the eighteenth century *The Tenth Muse* was reported to be in the library of George III.[3]

Thus, acclaimed and appreciated,[4] the first book of original English poetry written in America had been published, and it showed characteristics that were to stay with American poetry for a long time to come: an acceptance and use of the English poetic tradition and the modification of the tradition by dressing it in the "home-spun cloth" of American experience.

PART II

THE ANDOVER POEMS

THE ANDOVER POEMS

Even while the Bradstreets were moving to Ipswich, the General Court had given the order of March, 1635, that "the Land about Cochichowicke shalbe reserved for an inland plantacion" and in September of 1638 Simon Bradstreet, Samuel Dudley, Daniel Denison, John Woodbridge, and eight others were "allowed (upon their petition) to begin a plantation at Merrimack,"[1] the name given to the area.

The Bradstreets did not immediately move to the new settlement. But with the depression of the the 1640's when "the sudden fall of land and cattle, and the scarcity of foreign commodities, and money, &c. with the thin access of people from England, put many into an unsettled frame of spirit,"[2] the agricultural possibilities of the Merrimack plantations must have appeared more favorable. In May of 1643, Governor Winthrop remarked in his journal that "about this time two plantations began to be settled upon Merrimack, Pentucket called Haverill, and Cochichawick called Andover." In September, 1644, he recorded that two churches were to be gathered — at Haverhill and at Andover — and a year later, in October, 1645, the church at Andover was formally organized with John Woodbridge as pastor.

Andover, later known as North Andover, to which the Bradstreets moved in the mid-1640's, differed from Ipswich in several ways.[3] Ipswich had become by 1642 the second largest settlement in the colony. Moreover, it was accessible to the sea. Samuel Maverick reported about 1660 in his *Briefe Discription of New England* that Ipswich lay "at the head of Agawame River, as farr up as Vessells cane come."[4] Andover, on the other hand, was from the beginning described as an inland plantation lying in one of the best agricultural districts in the state. Maverick wrote, "Fouer Leagues up this River [the

77

Merrimack] is Haverell, a pretty Toune & a few miles higher
is the Toune of Andover both these Tounes subsist by Husban-
dry."[5] Edward Johnson around 1650 recorded that Andover
was a place "well fitted for the husbandmans hand, were it
not that the remoteness of the place from Towns of trade,
bringeth some inconveniences upon the planters, who are in-
forced to carry their corn far to market."[6] Ellis records that
"the principal part of the town" was "near the meeting-house,
though the houses were too far apart to form much of a
village."[7] This was consistent with the predominantly
agricultural nature of Andover. Many years later in 1810
Timothy Dwight described North Andover as

> a very beautiful piece of ground. Its surface is
> elegantly undulating, and its soil in an eminent
> degree fertile. The meadows are numerous, large,
> and of the first quality. The groves, charmingly in-
> terspersed, are tall and thrifty. The landscape, every
> where varied, neat, and cheerful, is also, every where
> rich.
> This Parish is a mere collection of plantations,
> without any thing like a village. The houses are
> generally very good: the barns, large and well built.
> Upon the whole, Andover is one of the best far-
> ming Towns in Eastern Massachusetts.[8]

Spatially, then, the new town of Andover differed from the
more closely built town of Ipswich. Because of the scattered
nature of the village, the exchange of talk and news would be
more difficult, and each family would be put more upon its
own resources than in Ipswich. Thus into the poet's life in the
mid-1640's were introduced a physical and social change. She
was placed in an environment even more rural than that of
Ipswich. She was farther from the political and commercial
center of the colony, and she was placed in a society which
must have been forced to rely more closely on the family group
than the more worldly society of Ipswich.

Did this change affect her work? It is not possible to ascer-
tain with certainty how much of *The Tenth Muse* was written

before the move to Andover, but those poems that are dated were, and most of the others show characteristics of her earlier period. The great rift that all critics have noted in her work between the early public poems and the later personal poems is located at about this time. The poems of *The Tenth Muse* were worldly in the sense that they dealt with the ideas typical of the time and of the active world around Anne Bradstreet. The later poems, the Andover group, are quite different in character.

Anne Bradstreet, as has been shown, was always sensitive to her surroundings, and the environment of Andover emphasized family relationships and rural isolation. These became strong motifs in her later poetry, which was written with her family in mind and with the theme of rural isolation transformed to contemplation of nature. To these two motifs was added a theme which had been present in the Ipswich poetry especially in "Old Age," that of the spirit's struggle with the world on the way to the heavenly Kingdom. In the later work the inner argument replaces earlier, more pragmatic, concerns.

We shall see in the later poems an expression of the Christian spirit in combat with the flesh, a turning to God in times of affliction, and an attempt to view all nature as an expression of the glory of God. The increasing emphasis on religion may have come anyway as an evidence of advancing age and seriousness, but it is possible that the change came at least in part from the move to Andover.

Even before the move, however, an event occurred which had a sobering effect upon the poet — the death of her mother, Dorothy Dudley, in December, 1643. On that occasion she wrote an "Epitaph." The epitaph differs from the three earlier elegies in being on a person known and loved by the poet, and the warmth of the poet's feeling for her subject penetrates the outwardly objective description. Otherwise, the "worthy matron of unspotted life" resembles the character sketches her daughter had drawn in the quaternions, becoming an exemplary New England housewife and mother.[9] As in the early elegies, Anne Bradstreet does not promise her subject heavenly bliss. Rather, she gives her worldly remembrance: She "of all her Children, Children liv'd to see,/ Then dying, left a blessed memory."

It was after the death of her mother and the criticism of around 1643, that Anne Bradstreet turned away from the witty, sometimes humorous, sometimes satiric, poetry she had written earlier, moving into the high seriousness of the later work. Two poems from *The Tenth Muse* introduce the period.

One is "David's Lamention for Saul and Jonathan," a close paraphrase of 2 Samuel 1:19. Although Anne Bradstreet employed Biblical paraphrase within other poems, this is the only poem that is no more than paraphrase without any frame to give an extra dimension of meaning. Elizabeth Wade White explains it as a poem deploring the execution of Charles I, like Saul an anointed king, an event which shocked many Puritans.[10] Moreover, Hooke in his sermon of 1650, which Anne Bradstreet seems to have read, pointed out the virtue of sympathizing not only with one's friends and relations, but pointed out that "David sympathizeth with his very enemies."[11]

The second poem of the period 1643-1650, "The Vanity of all worldly things," gracefully asserts the theme that though all things of this world perish, there remains a greater good. The poem is well executed, but Anne Bradstreet would restate its theme with greater tension in "The Flesh and the Spirit," "Contemplations," and her later elegies. Coming after the vigorous and worldly poetry of the early 1640's, and probably after the move to Andover, it signals a low point in Anne Bradstreet's usually resilient spirit and marks the encroachment of the shadow that was to fall between the poet and her celebration of the world.

CHAPTER 7
THE FLESH AND THE SPIRIT

The great period of Anne Bradstreet's devotional poetry began inauspiciously with a notebook she kept during the years 1656-1657 and 1661-1662. The notebook describes her progress as a spiritual pilgrim from childhood until what she thought in 1656 might be her deathbed. Fearing to die without the chance of giving a last word of advice to her children, she composed her thoughts in a journal designed to give her children the "spiritual advantage" of her experience. The journal stresses her spiritual doubts and the bodily afflictions given by God as chastisement for her frequent falling into the snares of the world. The prose states the themes that would preoccupy her in the major poetry of the Andover period. The poetry represents the first important influence of the metrical Psalms on her work.

Since childhood Anne Bradstreet had listened to the singing of metrical Psalms; both in the old world and the new she had heard the versions by Sternhold and Hopkins which were appended to the Anglican *Book of Common Prayer* and sung by the congregations in the Church of England and the Puritan churches in America. After 1640 New England had her own version, translated by her own ministers and printed at Boston as the first book off the first press of New England. The poet doubtless shared the excitement of the other colonists when they received the new versions of the *Bay Psalm Book* and learned to sing them in the congregations. For her, the metrical Psalms offered another form for poetry, to be used when the appropriate occasion came. It did not come, as far as her surviving poetry indicates, until 1656, when she was confined with what she thought might be a fatal illness. Lest she die without giving her children the benefit of her recollection of God's "dealing" with her from childhood to the present

day, she set down her experiences in a notebook. The opening
letter records the various chastisements sent by God when her
heart strayed from his service. The afflictions she recites in-
clude various illnesses and the coming to a new world against
which her "heart rose." After the biographical letter, the jour-
nal continues with entries in both poetry and prose concerning
the current illness and her spiritual doubts. She closed the first
phase of the notebook September 30, 1657. After that, she
remained in good health for four years, during which she made
no entries. She resumed the notebook in May 1661, when she
was once more ill. By June, she recovered her health and wrote
a poem of thanksgiving. The remaining poems of 1661-1662
concern the illnesses and recovery of her husband and
daughter, her son's return from England, and her husband's
going to England and returning.

The journal represents the kind of record that many
Puritans kept of their spiritual progress. Moreover, in order to
become a member of the church, first at Boston, then at
Ipswich, Mistress Bradstreet had to recite the kind of life
history contained in the notebook — the being overtaken by
sin, the period of remorse, and the subsequent turning back to
God, who fills the sinner with certainty of justification. The
times of remorse and renewed sense of grace occurred, for
Anne Bradstreet, during periods of physical stress. Hence, il-
lnesses along with spiritual doubts, past and present, play an
important part in her journal.

The emphasis on illness in the notebook of 1656-1662 has
led many commentators to remark on the poet's frail health or
even her "chronic invalidism." The notebook was indeed
written during illness, but the poet wrote of her previous trials
in order to show God's "gracious" dealing with her. The
notebook does not report a lifetime of poor health; on the con-
trary, her entries could be the reaction of one who has enjoyed
considerable good health and is impatient under confinement.[1]

In keeping with her strong sense of poetic decorum, Anne
Bradstreet used the stanza forms of the metrical Psalms only
for poems concerning illness or other affliction or poems ad-
dressed to God in prayer or praise. The meter of the Psalms,

both in the Sternhold-Hopkins version and in the Bay Psalm Book, was most often iambic tetrameter, sometimes alternating with three-foot lines, the ancient ballad meter. All Bradstreet's poems in this form, with one exception, are to be found in the notebook of 1656-1662. The poet uses quatrains of both the open (abcb) and closed (abab) rhyme schemes. In the poems of 1656-1657, she generally rhymed all four lines *abab*; in those of 1661-1662, she almost invariably rhymed only two lines, *abcb*. She gives no clues as to why her quatrains underwent this loosening of form. But, since the poems were conceived as private ones, perhaps she did not feel the need to polish them as carefully as those that were to be passed around. Even in the first group, however, she is somewhat careless with rhyme.

At times she comes close to the consonant or vowel rhymes of more modern poetry, as in the best of her devotional poems, "As spring the winter doth succeed." In her use of "near-rhyme" she foreshadows Emily Dickinson, who also based her metrics on the hymnal.

Despite the fact that she used the rhythms of the Psalms, so rich in metaphor, Anne Bradstreet's devotional poems contain little imagery. Most are direct statements, straightforward appeals to God or acknowledgement of help in sorrow, or descriptions of discomfort. Some stanzas are so direct they remind us of the anatomical conversations of the four Humours:

> My burning flesh in sweat did boyle,
> My aking head did break;
> From side to side for ease I toyle,
> So faint I could not speak.

Others, though still written more out of piety than art, bear a clear music. In this they may be contrasted with their model, for the versification of the *Bay Psalm Book* is noted for awkward inversions of syntax. Two of Bradstreet's poems of prayer stand out as especially fine. One is that of May 13, 1657, which begins:

> As spring the winter doth succeed,
> And leaves the naked Trees doe dresse,
> The earth all black is cloth'd in green;
> At sun-shine each their joy expresse.

The other is the fervent prayer for the protection of her husband upon his going to England in January 1662. It contains the last of the poet's political allusions, for her husband's mission was to move King Charles II to grant to the colony its ancient patent and former privileges. Mistress Bradstreet mentions Simon's important business:

> Unto thy work he hath in hand,
> Lord, graunt Thou good Successe
> And favour in their eyes, to whom
> He shall make his Addresse.

Then follow the moving lines by the gentlewoman looking out at the bleak wintry woods:

> Remember, Lord, thy folk whom thou
> To wildernesse hast brought:
> Let not thine own Inheritance
> Bee sold away for Nought.

For the most part, however, the value of the notebook lies outside the poetry, in its insight into the nature of Anne Bradstreet's faith and her view of the meaning of affliction. Besides containing biographical comments, the notebook shows her concept of God, not as a God of wrath, but as a father who chastizes his children in order to save them. It shows her following the Puritan tendency to recite the events of her own life as a testimony of God's doings for the benefit of her children, and it indicates once again her devotion to her family. The prose is much better than the poetry, and in it, with her usual candor, Anne Bradstreet describes her doubts and hesitations. The conclusion of the introductory letter, in particular, speaks in a rush of direct and heartfelt statements, and it exemplifies the spiritual struggle important to all Puritans. She was to express that struggle poetically in "The Flesh and the Spirit." Both the theme of that poem and its tetrameter rhythm were foreshadowed in the notebook of 1656-1657.

For the Puritan the struggle in the world seemed lost to Puritan principles, in England at least, in the 1630's, when the great immigration to New England began. This seeming loss, and the turn of events of the early forties, and the projected continuation of the battle to the final overthrow of Pope and Turk was dealt with by Anne Bradstreet in "Old England and New." But she also wrote of the inner struggle, between the spirit, with its affinity to the next world, and the flesh, with its relation to the concrete and visible. Anne Bradstreet's version of this familiar Christian theme, titled "The Flesh and the Spirit," is probably her most definite statement of Christian hope. At the same time it is probably her strongest assertion of doubt of the reality of the insubstantial.

It is typical of Anne Bradstreet's writing that there is a statement of belief and a counter-current of emotional disagreement running against it. The counter-current may be expressed — sometimes wittily, as in her comments on men and women; more often it is implied in the tone or emotional content. In "The Flesh and the Spirit," Anne Bradstreet adopted a device which enabled her to express both the belief and the counter-belief in explicit terms. As in her quaternions, she turned to the debate form, which is admirably suited to this particular subject, since in no better way than through the voice of a character could Anne Bradstreet express the doubts that she genuinely felt. The two sisters who debated "close by the Banks of *Lacrim* flood" may be taken as representative of two aspects of the nature of Anne Bradstreet herself.

The immediate idea for a contest between the two sisters may have come from a similar debate in one of Francis Quarles' "Emblemes" (Book III, No. 14). In that poem Quarles shows a grim sister Spirit who takes pleasure in pointing out Death with his two-edged sword and the awful day of Doom in which "Fiends, with knotted whips of flaming wire," torture poor souls. Sister Flesh reproaches Spirit for her enjoyment of tortures and describes instead the shapes and colors of the visible world. The sisters of Bradstreet's debate are both more convincing in their depiction of the joys of this world and the next. Sister Spirit does not dwell on death at all, but speaks of the glories of the invisible kingdom; Sister Flesh praises the good that may be won in this world through action.

The structure of Bradstreet's poem is simple. Flesh speaks first, Spirit replies, and there the poem ends. Almost half of the argument of Flesh is devoted to a criticism of Spirit rather than a list of the pleasures sought by Flesh. The basis of the criticism is that Spirit believes in what is insubstantial. "Art fancy sick, or turn'd a Sot,/ To catch at shadowes which are not?" Flesh caustically asks her sister. Bradstreet's own distrust of the invisible, or at least her desire for concrete evidence, is suggested in some of the passages in the notebook, for example the entry of August 28, 1656, where she says: "O let me ever see Thee that Art invisible, and I shall not bee unwilling to come."

Though the main argument of Flesh is based on this criticism of the Spirit, Flesh does have her own lures. These are first of all honor, which leads to fame, which can make one immortal in this world. Honor and fame are followed by riches and pleasure. An interesting thing about these temptations of Flesh is that they are not expressed as vicious in any way. Pleasure is not described in the way that Bradstreet described the pastimes of the "*Brittish*, bruitish Cavaleer" for example. Pleasure is hardly dwelt on by Flesh at all, and may even be perfectly innocent pleasure, since all Flesh says is "Affect's thou pleasure? take thy fill,/ Earth hath enough of what you will." Moreover, these worldly attainments of honor, riches, and pleasure are to be gained in a sound Puritan manner, according to Sister Flesh. They are to be had by work. Flesh introduces them by the words "Come, come, Ile shew unto thy sence,/ Industry hath its recompence." Doubtless this rather high-minded Sister Flesh who worked hard for worldly goods bore some resemblance to many Puritans, including Mistress Bradstreet, who was herself very conscious of fame and who said in a letter of the notebook: "The Lord knowes I dare not desire that health that somtimes I have had, least my heart should bee drawn from him, and sett upon the world."

Though Spirit has only scorn for the "unregenerate" Flesh who cannot see the values of the invisible, Flesh at times has succeeded in tempting the Spirit. Spirit admits

> Thy flatt'ring shews Ile trust no more.
> How oft thy slave, hast thou me made,
> When I believ'd, what thou hast said,
> And never had more cause of woe
> Then when I did what thou bad'st doe.

We need only remember the poet's statement in the notebook that God "hath never suffered me long to sitt loose from him, but by one affliction or other hath made me look home, and search what was amisse — so usually thus it hath been with me that I have no sooner felt my heart out of order, but I have expected correction for it, which most commonly hath been upon my own person," to realize that Anne Bradstreet doubtless here refers to personal experience. But Spirit too has her positive possessions. These are above the "dull Capacity" of Flesh. The eye of Spirit is able to "pierce the heavens, and see/ What is Invisible." What Spirit sees is the vision of the New Jerusalem described in Revelation, with its duplication in a higher sphere of worldly charms — its walls of Jasper, gates of Pearl, streets of Gold, all lit by the glory proceeding from God.

The main lines of the argument then, between Flesh and Spirit, revolve around the reality of the Christian idea of the life after death, and only secondarily around the pleasures of the Flesh, which are regarded as hindrances to the contemplation of more eternal, but similar, pleasures in the next world. As Spirit says:

> My thoughts do yield me more content
> Then can thy hours in pleasure spent.
> Nor are they shadows which I catch,
> Nor fancies vain at which I snatch.

For Anne Bradstreet, the main struggle in the spiritual combat, as expounded in "The Flesh and the Spirit" and the opening letter of her notebook is with religious doubt. For her, the struggle continues even though she feels assured of her justification, for she is explicit in the letter that she regards herself as one of the elect. She reports that God "hath not left me altogether without the wittnes of his holy spirit, who hath oft given mee his word and sett to his Seal that it shall bee well with me. I have somtimes tasted of that hidden Manna that the world knowes not, and have sett up my Ebenezer, and have resolved with myself that against such a promis, such tasts of sweetnes, the Gates of Hell shall never prevail." Even without this written assurance, we know that she must have received some evidence of her justification in order to become a member of the church at Boston and again at Ipswich.

Despite her assurance of being one of the elect, however, Anne Bradstreet wrote: "I have often been perplexed that I have not found that constant Joy in my Pilgrimage and refreshing which I supposed most of the servants of God have." Her doubt revolved around four questions — whether there is a God, whether the God she worships is the true God, whether the Popish religion may not be the true one, and whether members of other Protestant sects may not be right.

First, as to the existence of God, she says: "Many times hath Satan troubled me concerning the verity of the scriptures, many times by Atheisme how I could know whether there was a God; I never saw any miracles to confirm me, and those which I read of how did I know but they were feigned." Her answer is based on reason: "That there is a God my Reason would soon tell me by the wondrous workes that I see, the vast frame of the Heaven and the Earth, the order of all things, night and day, Summer and Winter, Spring and Autumne, the dayly providing for this great houshold upon the Earth, the preserving and directing of All to its proper end. The consideration of these things would with amazement certainly resolve me that there is an Eternall Being."

Having conceded that there is an Eternal Being, Anne Bradstreet asks her second question: "But how should I know he is such a God as I worship in Trinity, and such a Saviour as I rely upon? tho: this hath thousands of Times been suggested to mee, yet God hath helped me over." Her answer to this question is that God must have revealed himself in his word, and the scriptures must be the word of God. Why? She gives several empirical reasons: (1) she has found "that operation by it that no humane Invention can work upon the Soul," (2) she recalls that judgements have fallen on those who have scorned it, (3) it has been preserved through the ages in spite of tyrants and enemies, (4) no other story shows "the beginnings of Times, and how the world came to bee as wee see," (5) the prophesies of the scriptures are fulfilled, which could not have been foreseen so far in advance by anyone but God.

Having thus assured herself that she worships the true God and that the scriptures are divine, she asks another question: "Why may not the Popish Religion bee the right? They have the same God, the same Christ, the same word: they only enterprett it one way, wee another."

This is not the first time such a question was asked in the colony. Winthrop recorded that in July, 1631, he, Dudley, "and Mr. Nowell, the elder of the congregation at Boston, went to Watertown to confer with Mr. Phillips, the pastor, and Mr. Brown, the elder of the congregation there, about an opinion, which they had published, that the churches of Rome were true churches."[2] In this case there was a debate, and the opinion was considered an error. However, Mr. Brown persisted in his belief. Again the three emissaries went to Watertown. This time they reconciled the congregation, and it "agreed to seek God in a day of humiliation."[3] Doubtless the colonists in general and the Dudley family in particular found much to talk about in the doings at Watertown.

Winthrop does not record the arguments he and his fellows advanced against the Roman churches, but Anne Bradstreet gives hers. First, she denounces "the vain fooleries that are in their Religion," meaning, of course, the vestments and ceremonies against which she wrote in "A Dialogue between Old England and New." Second, she objects to "their lying miracles." Third, she charges the Catholics with the "cruell persecutions of the Saints, which admitt were they as they terme them, yet not so to bee dealt withall." Probably her knowledge of these persecutions came from Foxe's *Book of*

Martyrs, a most popular history during this period. Foxe told
the sufferings of the Protestant martyrs in great detail, and the
book's many engravings show their horrible deaths, mostly
by burning. Bradstreet's comment that the saints, even had
they been the heretics that the Catholics called them, should
not have been so treated, contrasts with her wish that the
"Popish, hellish miscreants" of Ireland might "swill in bloud
untill they burst." In both cases, however, she is reacting to
stories of atrocities. Those coming from Ireland at the time
were extremely gruesome, and her more humane view as
regards the Protestant martyrs, is perhaps closer to her usual
character. At any rate, having considered the ceremonies,
superstitions, and persecutions she associated with the Church
of Rome, Bradstreet had little struggle in disposing of this par-
ticular doubt.

Her fourth question was harder to answer. "But some new
Troubles I have had since the world has been filled with
Blasphemy, and Sectaries, and some who have been accounted
sincere Christians have been carried away with them, that
somtimes I have said, Is there Faith upon the earth? and I have
not known what to think." Anne Hutchinson, though
Bradstreet does not mention her, was a sincere Christian, as
was Roger Williams; so were others, who denied the value of
infant baptism. And personal acquaintance with such heretics
probably made this question the hardest for Anne Bradstreet.
Her answer marks a return to the argument of faith, which
was absent in the beginning of her series of questions:

> But then I have remembered the words of Christ that
> so it must bee, and that, if it were possible, the very
> elect should be deceived. Behold, saith our Saviour, I
> have told you before. That hath stayed my heart, and
> I can now say, Return O my Soul, to thy Rest, upon
> this Rock Christ Jesus will I build my faith; and, if I
> perish, I perish.

Thus, turning from reason to faith, Anne Bradstreet ex-
presses her own intensely personal experience. It is a vital ex-
perience and central to much of the thinking of Christians. For

Bradstreet, the spiritual combat was a struggle with doubt. In her account of that struggle she relied on revelation through the scriptures and through observation and experience of nature — i.e., faith and reason — to uphold her conclusions.[4] We shall find further clues to the meaning of nature in the segment of her poetry next to be considered.

Tempus erit.

Emblematic figures from Francis Quarles' *Hieroglyphikes of the Life of Man*, 1638.

CHAPTER 8
CONTEMPLATIONS

Like others of her time, Anne Bradstreet knew the value of meditation and contemplation as spiritual aids. She begins her poem "The Flesh and the Spirit" by mentioning both practices:

Sister, quoth Flesh, what liv'st thou on
Nothing but Meditation?
Doth Contemplation feed thee so
Regardlessly to let earth goe?
Can Speculation satisfy
Notion without Reality?

In 1664 she began a series of prose *Meditations*, which, according to her son Simon, she continued working on until her death. And in the 1650's or 1660's, she composed the first important meditative poem written in America, giving it the title "Contemplations."[1]

The term "meditation" often refers to a formal spiritual exercise or series of exercises which were predominantly practiced by Catholic or Anglicans both on the Continent and in England. For the Puritan, meditation or contemplation up to the middle of the seventeenth century often meant merely the serious pondering of religious matters.[2] However, Anne Bradstreet's poem "Contemplations" reflects the methods of poets familiar with the more formal art or exercise. This art involved the use of all the powers of the soul: the memory coupled with the imagination, the understanding or reason, and the affections and the will. The memory was used to decide upon the subject of the meditation, which the imagination was to portray vividly in what was known as the "composition of place." The understanding might then draw out comparisons or analogies between the imagined scene and the spiritual condition of the meditator, or might through the vividness of the depicted scene involve the emotions or "affections." The scenes might be from stories of the Old or New Testaments or imaginary events like the terrors of Hell. The effort of the will to move the meditator toward virtuous acts or emotions demonstrated itself in the prayer or colloquy with which the meditation concluded.[3]

The Puritan minister Richard Baxter adapted these Catholic methods of meditation for the use of Puritans. His book, *The Saints Everlasting Rest*, stressed the importance of setting aside certain portions of each day or week for "the set and solemn acting of all the powers of the soul, To difference it from the common Meditation of Students, which is usually the meer employment of the Brain." The affections as well as the understanding were to be used in meditation — the feelings of love and joy, desire, hope and courage. Besides the understanding, and the affections, said Baxter, contemplation involves soliloquy with self and colloquy with God.[4]

St. Francis deSales had earlier summed up the possibilities of the soliloquy or colloquy: "It is good to use colloquies, or familiar talke, as it were somtime with God our Lord, somtime with our blessed Ladie, with the Angels, and persons represented in the mysterie which we meditate, with the Saints of heaven, with our selves, with our owne hart, with sinners, yea and with insensible creatures."[5]

During the last half of the seventeenth century, the creatures increasingly replaced the events of the incarnation in the composition of place in English meditative poetry.

Baxter took note of the trend:

> There is yet another way by which we may make our senses here serviceable to us; and that is, By comparing the objects of sense with the objects of faith; and so forcing sense to afford us that *Medium,* from whence we may conclude the transcendent worth of Glory, By arguing from sensitive delights as from the less to the greater... [6]

The thought that the creation is visible proof of the existence of God appeared repeatedly also in New England sermons:

> Can we, when we behold the stately theater of heaven
> and earth, conclude other but that the finger, arms,
> and wisdom of God hath been here, although we see
> not him that is invisible . . . ? Every creature in
> heaven and earth is a loud preacher of this truth.[7]

Meditation on the "stately theater" and its creatures could
best occur outdoors, the traditional scene being the field, in ac-
cord with the Biblical example of Isaac, who "went out to pray
in the field toward the evening." The Geneva Bible takes
cognizance of the place and the custom of meditation, saying
in the marginal note on this passage: "This was the exercise of
the godlike fathers to meditate Gods promisses & to pray for
the accomplishment thereof." The minister Thomas Shepard,
Anne Bradstreet's New England contemporary, thus recorded
his experience: "This I remember, I never went out to
meditate in the feelds, but I did find the Lord teaching me
somewhat of my selfe or himselfe or the vanity of the woorld
I never saw before; & hence I tooke out a little book I have
every day into the feelds & writ down what god taught me
least I should forget them."[8]

Anne Bradstreet mentions the soul's colloquy with God in a
poem written in 1662 during her "Solitary houres" in the
absence of her husband, where she says:

> And thy Abode tho'st made with me;
>   With Thee my Soul can talk
> In secrett places, Thee I find,
>   Where I do kneel or walk.

The "secret places" might well have been out among the
creatures of nature, for in the first line of "The Flesh and the
Spirit" she speaks of the "secret place where once I
stood/Close by the Banks of *Lacrim* flood." Here she may be
speaking of an actual stream, as well as punning on the Latin
word for "tears."

In "Contemplations" she closely follows one form of the
meditative poem as it was developed in the mid-seventeenth
century: The subject of the meditation may be one of the
creatures observed and described in its natural setting. The

"composition of place" involves, then, a description of this creature and its situation; the understanding develops from this creature various "verities;" and the colloquy concluding the meditation might be with God about the creature or with the creature itself. The meditative poem thus described moves in the direction of the didactic nature poem and ultimately toward one type of poem typical of the later Romantics. But at this state it is still closely related to the meditation and to another genre which was prominent in the seventeenth centurey and which paralleled the meditative tradition and finally blended with it. I refer here to emblematic literature.

Emblem books, popular in the seventeenth century on the Continent and later in England, consisted of pictures accompanied by a text, usually in verse but sometimes in prose. The text explained the symbols involved in the picture and drew a moral.[9] The emblems of Wither and Quarles were especially appealing to the Puritans. The emblem, with its three-fold structure of picture, the drawing of the analogy, and moral, runs close to the structure of the meditative poem.

A reader of the seventeenth century could hardly fail to be aware of both these ways of composing. Though Anne Bradstreet may or may not have read any books on the art of meditation as a method of spiritual exercise, her comments already cited show that she thought of meditation as a spiritual aid. Clearly she knew emblem literature; many of her prose meditations take the form of emblems, and she uses the word itself several times. "Meditation XL," in which she likens spring to an emblem of the resurrection (and which, incidentally, foreshadows the imagery of "As weary pilgrim") may serve as illustration. Other meditations (for example, IV and LXXII) involve even simpler analogies, which bear a picture-to-moral relationship.

The fact that Anne Bradstreet calls these aphorisms *Meditations Divine and morall,* yet follows the procedure of the emblem books in so many of them, indicates that she felt a close connection between meditation and emblems. Martz states that "what Miss Freeman says of the English Catholic emblem-books will hold also for Wither and Quarles: 'Their main purpose is the practice of meditation, and to this purpose the emblems are no more than contributory factors.' ''[10] The statement would also apply to some extent to Bradstreet in her *Meditations,* but even more strikingly in the poem "Contemplations."

"Contemplations" is a poem of thirty-three stanzas reflecting, throughout, the meditative and emblematic traditions. Beginning with a description of place, it moves through a series of commentaries on the objects seen, and it concludes with an apostrophe to Time. Within this broad structure, however, is a whole series of smaller meditative or emblematic poems which blend into one another. All together they state the double theme that the creatures of earth express the glory of God and are in many ways stronger and more lasting than man whose life is short and full of care; yet he alone of all the creatures may achieve immortal life.

The composition of place is established in the first two stanzas, which describe the glory of Autumn: "If so much excellence abide below;/How excellent is he that dwells on high?" Then the poem moves to a more detailed look at the scene, first at an oak tree, then at the sun. From each of these, "verities" are drawn, and at the close of stanza 7 the first movement of the poem comes to an end. The next two stanzas describe the poet's attempt to write poetry appropriate to the praise of God and how she is outdone by the grasshopper and the cricket.

The poem then shifts entirely to an imaginative scene which reminds us that the earlier meditations turned upon events in the life of Christ and other Biblical stories. In imagination the poet depicts various scenes of the Old Testament: the fall of Adam and Eve, Eve holding the infant Cain, the murder of Abel. These are all within the concept of presenting the matter to be meditated on to the eye of the mind. The conclusion of this section compares the shortness of life of modern man to that of his ancestors, a reminder that the idea of the decay of man since the Fall was still a vital one.

The idea of the shortness of man's life is carried on in the next group of stanzas (18-20) where the poet returns once more to the natural scene and, using the emblems of heavens, trees, and earth, comments on the mortality of the creatures. The following group (stanzas 21-25) observes the stream, calling it our "emblem."

> Thou Emblem true, of what I count the best,
> O could I lead my Rivolets to rest,
> So we may press to that vast mansion, ever blest.

Stanzas 29-32 describe the woes of mankind in general terms; within this group, stanza 31 contains the emblem of the mariner suddenly running into a storm, and the next stanza draws the moral that "Only above is found all with security."

There follows the last stanza of the poem, which addresses Time. Though this address occupies the usual position of the colloquy, it is closer to simple apostrophe or direct address. However, in using the form of direct address to a creature or abstraction, Anne Bradstreet is following the form of the meditative poem, which also concludes with an address, but she is using the form to draw a moral. Here she is not following the formal method of meditation, but is adapting the meditative poetry she has read to her purposes and fusing it with the emblematic practice of moralizing at the end of a poem. The address to Time draws the moral of the vanity of all things and the mortality and immortality of man that has been stressed throughout. Its couplet form sets it off from the rest of the poem:

> O Time the fatal wrack of mortal things,
> That draws oblivions curtains over kings,
> Their sumptuous monuments, men know them not,
> Their names without a Record are forgot,
> Their parts, their ports, their pomp's all laid in th'dust
> Nor wit nor gold, nor buildings scape times rust;
> But he whose name is grav'd in the white stone
> Shall last and shine when all of these are gone.

The whole poem might be read as a meditation, since it moves from a statement of subject — the inferring of excellence to God by looking at his creatures — within a description of the scene, through a detailed analysis of the scene or the pictorial element in terms of its analogies to moral truths, to the final address to Time. Within the long meditation are the shorter ones on the fishes and birds, with their moral implications, as well as partial meditations in which the pictorial is stressed, as in the descriptions of Adam and Eve, Cain and Abel. The poem may also be read as a series of short emblematic poems. Anne Bradstreet is apparently familiar with both traditions and in her usual eclectic way has used them for her purposes.

In doing so she has made excellent structural use of her stanza form. The stanza is iambic pentameter and the rhyme is that of a quatrain, followed by a triplet, *ababccc*. The last line of each stanza is hexameter. The rhyme scheme lends itself to a division in the stanza between the quatrain and triplet, and Anne Bradstreet has made full use of this natural division.

Almost every stanza observes the division into four lines and three by a break in syntax and a break in context. The quatrain paints the picture or sets the scene or asks the question. The triplet interprets the picture or states the moral lesson or draws out the verities of the picture. Thus the individual stanza repeats in small space what the larger groups of stanzas do as a group, and what the whole poem does. The poem is as intricately put together as a nest of boxes.

Her method is well illustrated in the presentation of the stream in stanzas 21-23, the last of which contains a colloquy, though not of the strictly meditative type, with the emblem. Another group of stanzas, more abstract in language, which illustrate the stanzaic structure rather compactly are 18 to 20:

18

When I behold the heavens as in their prime,
And then the earth (though old) stil clad in green,
The stones and trees, insensible of time,
Nor age nor wrinkle on their front are seen;
If winter come, and greeness then do fade,
A Spring returns, and they more youthfull made;
But Man grows old, lies down, remains where once he's
   laid.

19

By birth more noble than those creatures all,
Yet seems by nature and by custome curs'd,
No sooner born, but grief and care makes fall
That state obliterate he had at first:
Nor youth, nor strength, nor wisdom spring again
Nor habitations long their names retain,
And in oblivion to the final day remain.

20

Shall I then praise the heavens, the trees, the earth
Because their beauty and their strength last longer
Shall I wish there, or never to had birth
Because they're bigger, & their bodyes stronger?
Nay, they shall darken, perish, fade and dye,
And when unmade, so ever shall they lye,
But man was made for endless immortality.

Here the division within the stanzas is clear, the emblem or picture of heavens, earth, and trees being used as a contrast to the state of man, the contrast being made between the quatrain and the triplet of the first and last stanzas, and argued in both parts of the central stanza. Together the three stanzas state the theme of the whole series of contemplations. The stanza form, then, in which the last three lines comment on the first four, is particularly well adapted to a contemplative poem, and with the added foot in the last line of each stanza adds the leisurely pace which seems right for the mood.

Bradstreet's stanza may be contrasted with that of John Rogers, who wrote a poetical address to the author published in the second edition of her book. Rogers probably used her form as a model, but his quatrain often runs into the triplet and the whole structure of his poem is less dense.

Bradstreet's use of the stanza differs, too, from that of Phineas Fletcher in *The Purple Island*, a poem which some have claimed influenced the poet in her choice of form.[11] *The Purple Island* is descriptive and narrative rather than contemplative; so that the possibility of one part of the stanza commenting on the other does not often arise. What we find in Fletcher is the same frequent break in syntax between the two parts of the stanza, though occasionally he runs the fourth line over into the fifth (as in XII, 63), but there is usually no break in context. The description or narrative continues through the stanza, and it would not matter whether a particular statement occurred in the quatrain or the triplet.

Whatever influence Anne Bradstreet received from Fletcher doubtless came by way of Francis Quarles' *Emblemes and Hieroglyphikes,* 1639. Quarles, in writing his emblems, broke away from his earlier heroic couplets to experiment with various stanza forms suggested to him by Fletcher. For "Hierogliph. II" and several "Emblemes" (I.4; IV.1; IV.12; V.9) he used the stanza that Anne Bradstreet later adopted, including her separation of the quatrain and triplet into statement and comment. Her rhythms in "Contemplations" are close to those of "Hieroglyph. II," stanza 6:

> But why should Man, the Lord of Creatures, want
> That priviledge which Plants and Beasts obtaine?
> Beasts bring forth Beasts, the Plant a perfect Plant;
> And every like brings forth her like againe:
> Shall fowles, and fishes, beasts and plants convey
> Life to their issue? And Man lesse than they?
> Shall these get living soules? And Man, dead lumps of
>   clay?

Although Bradstreet adopted the Spenserian stanza, as modified by Fletcher and Quarles, her poem is free of the classical and pastoral characters and allusions that abound in the older poets. She mentions only Phoebus, the sun, and Philomel, a bird, and refers to "*Thetis* house" and "*Neptun's* glassie Hall" in connection with river and sea. Except in the passage based on the Old Testament, her characters are the living things around her, to whom she sometimes speaks. The central character is the poet herself with all her reactions to nature; thus she takes a step in the direction of the poet-centered verse of the Romantics. As with the Romantics, her language, stripped of classical trappings, is direct and simple.

It represents the plain style at its best. There are a few metaphors, but they are understated and inconspicuous, not the bringing together of startling disparates to make a conspicuous conceit. Such a metaphor as

> The stones and trees, insensible of time,
> Nor age nor wrinkle on their front are seen

blends so inconspicuously into its stanza that the fact of metaphor is scarcely noticed. By means of the technique of the emblem, metaphor becomes analyzed into its terms; it is spread from the compactness of the single image into the two parallel images of the simile. For example, stanza 31 draws a picture of a mariner who "sings merrily and steers his bark with ease" until he runs into a storm.The next stanza describes the man "who saileth in this world of pleasure." There is comparison of the two situations in these stanzas rather than identification. The man in the world is not said to *be* a mariner, as would have occurred in a metaphor of the metaphysical variety, but is a distinct man who is compared with the mariner. Thus the emblem, though itself a comparison, enables Anne Bradstreet to write in a direct style, even when she says that there are a "thousand fancies buzzing in my brain." (Stanza 26)

The question arises as to how her attitude toward nature in "Contemplations" compares with her earlier style and attitude toward nature in "The Four Seasons." In both these works, nature is more than a convention; the poet obviously delights in contemplating it. The opening stanza of "Contemplations" indicates her relish of the scene:

> Some time now past in the Autumnal Tide,
> When *Phoebus* wanted but one hour to bed,
> The trees all richly clad, yet void of pride,
> Where gilded o're by his rich golden head.
> Their leaves & fruits seem'd painted, but was true
> Of green, of red, of yellow, mixed hew.
> Rapt were my sences at this delectable view.

She feels almost a Romantic involvement. But both here and in "The Four Seasons" the enjoyment of nature is kept subor-

dinate to the main purpose of the poem. Utility remains
always in the background of Puritan poetry, and in the case of
Anne Bradstreet, makes a distinction between her comprehen-
sion of nature and that of the Romantics. Utility also causes
the difference between the treatment of nature in the two
poems we are now considering.

"The Four Seasons" was part of a long encyclopaedic
poem, designed to convey useful knowledge, and a description
of the four seasons was part of knowledge and legitimately
included. As a consequence, "The Four Seasons," though it
contains other elements, in large part directly describes
the poet's surroundings. "Contemplations" too contains
description, but it does not aim at conveying useful earthly
knowledge. It is a poem in which the poet observes, meditates,
and draws conclusions, and which is written down as a descrip-
tion of her process of meditation for the benefit of the reader,
or, as Shepard wrote, lest the writer forget what God hath
taught. A poet following two such different purposes will write
a different kind of poem, even though the natural scene and
the poet's delight in it remain the same. "Contemplations" is
an attempt to find the truth through the visible. Nature can be
used as a means of contemplating the glory of God, who is
beyond nature and separate from it. But nature itself can be
admired because through it God makes a part of his glory visi-
ble to mortal eyes. "Contemplations" embraces both these
ideas — the invisible glory behind nature and the visible and
lesser glory that stands as emblem of the greater. The poem
balances on the tension between the two kinds of glory:
through most of the poem the author concentrates on visible
nature.

But her use of nature, however much she enjoys it, is con-
stantly subject to the restraint of the emblematic moral pur-
pose. Certain portions of the poem show an unhampered
delight in nature for several lines at a time, thus foreshadowing
the age to come. But always for Anne Bradstreet God is the
source of order and meaning; landscape in her poems is order-
ly and clearly divided into its separate parts. Nature is not wild
or mingled as in Romantic poetry. Nor does nature reflect her

feelings — she distinguishes between herself and her surroundings. Poetry for her could never become merely "self-expression" for always behind it lies the concept of utility.

Nevertheless, in "Contemplations" Bradstreet discloses a love of nature in its milder aspects. In doing so, she continues the argument between the Flesh and the Spirit. And in it, she poses the best resolution of the argument; in the joy of contemplating nature she can also grow closer to the invisible spirit behind the veil. Yet this, her most serene poem, is not without tension. The Flesh can glorify nature, can aptly describe the autumn scene so gilded and colored with green, red, and yellow that it appears to be the product of *man's* hand — the leaves and fruit "seem'd painted." Yet when it is time to glorify the Creator, her "mazed Muse" breaks down with the cry "But Ah, and Ah, again, my imbecility." Even the "merry grasshopper" and "black clad Cricket" can praise their maker; while the poet "as mute, can warble forth no higher layes"[12] and turns from what is at hand to the older kind of meditation, the calling forth of scenes from the Old Testament. She calls on "fancy" to depict Adam and Eve and their children. Through them she introduces the motif that dominates the second half of the poem, the decay of all created things in contrast to the immortality of those whose names are "graved in the white stone." Anne Bradstreet's muse turned to God when the flesh was afflicted, but seldom at other times. Even in this poem of praise for God's world, the poet, rather than God or nature, stands at the center of the poem, and her accent is more on the world than on its Creator. With the "sinfull creature" of stanza 30, for whom not "all his losses, crosses and vexation,/In weight, in frequency and long duration/Can make him deeply groan for that divine Translation," Anne Bradstreet preferred the visible to that which she could not see.[13] The complexity of the metaphor in "Contemplations" is testified to by a number of recent studies indicating various metaphorical and typological bases for the organization of the poem. Such arrangements of imagery, of course, overlie the essentially formal basis of meditation that has been described above.

Quite different in substance as in form are the prose *Meditations* which she began in March of 1664. Many of the *Meditations* take the form of emblems, enough to indicate that she associated the emblem form with meditation. Some of these stop at rather simple metaphors, numbers 19 and 23, for example. In the first, corn which must be milled before being made into bread is likened to God's servants who must be ground with grief and affliction; in the second, Satan is compared to an Angler who uses different baits for different fish. In some of the other longer, more complex *Meditations*, we can still perceive the argument as taking off from an actual picture, such as might be found in the emblem books which Anne Bradstreet had no doubt perused. Number 50, which begins with an image of the sun covered by a cloud, represents this more complex form. Still other meditations contain no picture but are aphorisms or short aphoristic essays in the Baconian manner. The *Meditations* represent in Anne Bradstreet's work the more general concept of meditation as serious thoughts about a subject; in them she does not employ the more formal method of "Contemplations." The subject varies widely from meditation to meditation, without the associative sequence or the tension generated by the poetry.

The *Meditations* reflect more closely the religious formulae of her time, and they accept such formulae without the questioning that went on in the prose of her notebooks. They are filled with observations on sin and the good Christian and the vanity of the world's goods. The lack of tension perhaps grows out of their purpose. In the opening letter to her son Simon, she explains that she is writing the *Meditations* as a legacy to him when she shall no longer be with him. The purpose, and to some extent the form itself, precludes the discussion of spiritual doubt, already set down in the notebook of 1657-1661. But even at this late time in her life, she reasserts her originality, as if still feeling some pang of the earlier disapproval. The words, "I have avoyded incroaching upon others conceptions, because I would leave you nothing but myne owne, though in value they fall short of all in this kind," echo her statement of twenty-two years before, that she would not steal from Du Bartas and her insistence in "The Prologue" that the carping tongues would say "it's stolen."

The *Meditations* are unquestionably drawn from real life. While some reflect Biblical assertions, putting them in contemporary settings, others are based directly on images of everyday affairs, common occupations, and family life — weather and seasons, fishing and farming, the human body, with its aging, burdens, and ailments, and the relations of mother and child. Those on the last mentioned subjects (numbers 10, 38, 39, 48, 61) are of special interest in giving an insight into Mistress Bradstreet's views on child-rearing. Notable is the modern idea that "diverse children have their different natures... those parents are wise that can fit their nurture according to their Nature." Number 21 uses imagery close to that the poet would use in the "Weary Pilgrim" of 1669. The prose is vigorous and varied in its structure, and the pieces themselves range from around three to twenty lines, growing longer as their author gains practice in the form.[14]

Thus, even while they often assert religious or moral commonplaces, the *Meditations* indicate that in the last years of her life, Anne Bradstreet continued as an observant and dedicated writer, willing to undertake and master new forms of expression. She asserts her individuality, her originality, in the introductory letter, and she expresses confidence that her work will be gratefully received and approved by her audience of one. In one more way, by composing her *Meditations,* the poet strives for worldly remembrance.

CHAPTER 9
THE FINAL ELEGIES

Anne Bradstreet's inner argument reached its climax in the poetry of her final years. There, in the poems of 1665-1669, she presents the argument of "The Flesh and the Spirit" with reference to actual occurences. The Flesh had argued for the visible against the invisible, for honor, riches, and pleasure. What the real woman wants is, more than riches, a home with its beloved comforts and memories; more than honor and pleasure, the lives of loved ones; and life itself. In these last poems Anne Bradstreet deals directly with these genuine and human desires, projecting the conflict that occurred within herself.

In the first of the series she is concerned with the loss of the visible. On July 10, 1666, the Bradstreet house in North Andover burned to the ground. Mistress Bradstreet with her usual care for her writings, must have snatched up the two notebooks containing her journal and her prose meditations as she rushed out-of-doors, for they were preserved. In her poem on the subject, she describes awakening to "shrieks of dreadfull voice" and going out to watch "the flame consume my dwelling place." Later as she passes the ruins, she re-creates the pleasant things that had been there:

Here stood that Trunk, and there that chest;
There lay that store I counted best:
My pleasant things in ashes lye,
And them behold no more shall I.
Under thy roof no guest shall sitt,
Nor at thy Table eat a bitt.
No pleasant tale shall 'ere be told,
Nor things recounted done of old.
No Candle 'ere shall shine in Thee,
Nor bridegroom's voice ere heard shall bee.

Thus she expresses her regret for the loss of her house and possessions and the loss of the physical setting for memories of events that happened in the house. But in answer to regret, she gives several arguments that well might have been spoken by the Spirit. There is no question that God was responsible for the holocaust:

> I blest his Name that gave and took,
> That layd my goods now in the dust.

But the doings of God should not be questioned:

> Yea so it was, and so 'twas just.

Besides

> It was his own: it was not mine;
> ffar be it that I should repine.

Yet she does proceed to repine in the next sixteen lines in describing the contents of the house. The progress of the poem becomes an inner dialogue, for she begins to chide her own heart, in the manner of the Spirit:

> And did thy wealth on earth abide?
> Didst fix thy hope on mouldring dust,
> The arm of flesh didst make thy trust?
> Raise up thy thoughts above the skye
> That dunghill mists away may flie.
> Thou hast an house on high erect,
> Fram'd by that mighty Architect,
> With glory richly furnished,
> Stands permanent tho: this bee fled.

The poem concludes with

> Farewell my Pelf, farewell my Store.
> The world no longer let me Love,
> My hope and Treasure lyes Above.

Regardless of the rational conclusion, and the reasonable argument that this was all God's property anyway and whatever God does is just, the poem contains a strong feeling of loss not fully compensated for by the hope of treasure that lies above.

This is even more true in the four elegies on her grandchildren and her daughter-in-law.

It was the custom in the Bay Colony to pin commemorative verses to the bier of one who had died. Copies of such verses were often passed out at the graveside or printed as a broadside. The writer of the elegy tried "not to offer something new but only to say what everyone knows"—[1] that is, he attempted to give an accurate portrayal of the life and virtues of the departed, as Anne Bradstreet had done in the elegy on Dorothy Dudley. Imagination did have a place in the funeral elegy, but only through the use of anagrams, conceits, and puns. The writer of a funeral elegy need not be a poet, and his lack of skill was covered by the inclusion of an apology for his artlessness and the declaration that his grief caused him to write. Anne Bradstreet's funeral elegies differ from those most often written in New England in several ways. They are without apology for the writer's lack of skill; they use few and gentle conceits; and the feeling expressed in them is intense and personal.

The two elegies by Anne Bradstreet which most closely fit the usual pattern of the New England funeral elegy were written earlier, that on the death of her mother in 1643, already discussed, and that of her father ten years later.

The poem on her father, is the more personal. It begins with an expression of her deep sense of obligation:

> By duty bound, and not by custome led
> To celebrate the praises of the dead,
> My mournfull mind, sore prest, in trembling verse
> Presents my Lamentations at his Herse,
> Who was my Father, Guide, Instructer too,
> To whom I ought whatever I could doe.

There follows one of the strangest apologies to be found among the New England funeral elegies — not an excuse for lack of skill, but a defense against the criticism she knew would come because she presumed to praise her father:

Nor is't Relation near my hand shall tye;
For who more cause to boast his worth then I?
Who heard or saw, observ'd or knew him better?
Or who alive then I, a greater debtor?
Let malice bite, and envy knaw its fill,
He was my Father, and Ile praise him still.

In *The Tenth Muse*, writing of Sidney, she had said:
Let then, none dis-allow of these my straines,
Which have the self-same blood yet in my veines.

In the second edition, she changed the second line of the couplet
to:

Whilst English blood yet runs within my veins.

This change was not made merely, as Augustine Jones and
others suggest, for reasons of decorum, but because of outright
criticism. The "carping tongues" had no doubt censured Anne
Bradstreet for the sin of pride in claiming relationship to the
subject of her praise, especially after the publication of her
book in 1650.[2] In 1653, freshly stung by their comments, she is
attempting to forestall similar criticism of praise of her il-
lustrious father by calling it in advance the product of malice
and envy. She goes on to counter another argument — that
there are plenty of others to praise so well known a man:

Nor was his name, or life lead so obscure
That pitty might some Trumpeters procure,
Who after death might make him falsely seem
Such as in life, no man could justly deem.
Well known and lov'd, where ere he liv'd, by most
Both in his native, and in foreign coast,
These to the world his merits could make known,
So needs no Testimonial from his own;
But now or never I must pay my Sum;
While others tell his worth, I'le not be dumb.

After this lengthy justification, the elegy describes her father's
virtues — patriotic and public and private.

An important change in this poem distinguishes it in yet
another way from the elegy on her mother and from the poems

in praise of Du Bartas, Sidney, and Elizabeth. For Thomas
Dudley, his daughter posits, for the first time in an elegy, the
Christian apotheosis:

> Ah happy Soul, 'mongst Saints and Angels blest,
> Who after all his toyle, is now at rest.

In such conclusion, the poem serves as a transition to the later
elegies. But there is one difference, and that is a subtle one of
tone. Here there is an unquestioning feeling of the rightness of
his death and undoubted resurrection. A graceful conceit
asserts that his death is "timely":

> Now fully ripe, as shock of wheat that's grown,
> Death as a Sickle hath him timely mown,
> And in celestial Barn hath hous'd him high,
> Where storms, nor showrs, nor ought can damnifie.
> His Generation serv'd, his labours cease;
> And to his Fathers gathered is in peace.

It is otherwise in the little poems on the death of her
grandchildren.

Of the four elegies written during Anne Bradstreet's final
poetic period, three were in commemoration of the deaths of
the three daughters and son of her eldest son Samuel; and the
fourth marked the death of their mother.

A strong note of personal bereavement runs through them,
and there is a tendency to interpret the deaths in relation to the
poet herself. The voice of the Spirit could argue rationally that
all her possessions were really God's and subject to recall, and
she could accept this, on a rational level at least. But what
could Spirit say when God, who was responsible for all things,
took away her dearest relatives? The argument extends over
the four elegies, and though they are dated over a period of
time, there is a singular unity in the theme and its develop-
ment.

The first poem on her grandchild Elizabeth who died in
August 1665, at the age of one and a half years is the least
resigned. In its poignancy and simplicity, it is one of the finest
of Bradstreet's family poems. In it Anne Bradstreet had the

good fortune or wit to use the "Contemplations" stanza, which is as well adapted to elegy as to meditative verse. The poem is only two stanzas long.

> Farewel dear babe, my hearts too much content,
> Farewel sweet babe, the pleasure of mine eye,
> Farewel fair flower that for a space was lent,
> Then ta'en away unto Eternity.
> Blest babe why should I once bewail thy fate,
> Or sigh thy dayes so soon were terminate;
> Sith thou art setled in an Everlasting state.
>
> By nature Trees do rot when they are grown.
> And Plumbs and Apples throughly ripe do fall,
> And Corn and grass are in their season mown,
> And time brings down what is both strong and tall.
> But plants new set to be eradicate,
> And buds new blown, to have so short a date,
> Is by his hand alone that guides nature and fate.

In the first line she admits that her heart is set too much upon one who is, after all, merely a creature of God, only lent for a short space, just as were her possessions in the poem on her house. In the triplet of the first stanza she asks as a question what should in most elegies become the apotheosis near the end. She asks why she should grieve since the child is now settled in an everlasting state. However, as in the poem on the burning of her house, she goes on in the next stanza to tell why she should grieve, and the feeling is closer to Herrick and the Cavaliers than to the usual funeral elegy of New England. That "time brings down what is both strong and tall" she has already expressed in the elegy on her father, and this is acceptable. But for "buds new blown, to have so short a date," [3] is a state of affairs she cannot justify. With Sylvester, whose book she read so many years before, she says merely that it is God's will.[4] In this poem there is no real reply to the Flesh that loves God's creatures.

The reply comes four years later in the elegy on her grandchild Anne Bradstreet, who died June 20, 1669. The reply is simply a strengthening of the two arguments suggested

but not developed in the earlier poem. First, she should not set
her heart on earthly things:

> How oft with disappointment have I met,
> When I on fading things my hopes have set?
> Experience might 'fore this have made me wise,
> To value things according to their price:
> Was ever stable joy yet found below?
> Or perfect bliss without mixture of woe.

Second, God's creatures are ephemeral and only lent:

> I knew she was but as a withering flour,
> That's here to day, perhaps gone in an hour;
> Like as a bubble, or the brittle glass,
> Or like a shadow turning as it was.
> More fool then I to look on that was lent,
> As if mine own, when thus impermanent.

There follows a touch of the world-weariness which was to
show up a little over two months later in "As weary pilgrim."

> Farewel dear child, thou ne're shall come to me,
> But yet a while, and I shall go to thee.

Then comes the ending, a proper statement of Christian com-
fort:

> Mean time my throbbing heart's chear'd up with this
> Thou with thy Saviour art in endless bliss.

This is a decorous Puritan poem, in which earthly values are
looked at in appropriate relation to eternal ones. But when the
third of Samuel's children, Simon, died in November of the
same year, Anne Bradstreet shows more of her usual tension.
Her elegy on Simon begins quietly enough:

> No sooner come, but gone, and fal'n asleep,
> Acquaintance short, yet parting caus'd us weep,
> Three flours, two scarcely blown, the last i'th'bud,
> Cropt by th' Almighties hand;...

But these lines, in simply stating how God has used his power,
become intensely ironic, especially when followed by "yet is he

good." In the situation she describes, God himself must be defended. She goes on with characteristically reluctant acceptance:

> With dreadful awe before him let's be mute,
> Such was his will, but why, let's not dispute,
> With humble hearts and mouths put in the dust,
> Let's say he's merciful as well as just.

If the word "say" is emphasized, the poem comes close to blasphemy. The goodness of God, though piously mouthed, seems to be weighed and found wanting. The last four lines of the poem are a quiet settling down after a near approach to criticism of God, if not in words, at least in feeling.

When a year later the mother of the three dead children also died, Anne Bradstreet wrote another elegy. Genuine grief moves through the opening lines, but the poem is closer to the usual New England elegy, and the bitterness of the poems on Elizabeth and Simon Bradstreet is missing. This poem even manages a conceit reminiscent of the metaphysical love poems:

> Thou being gone, she longer could not be,
> Because her Soul she'd sent along with thee.

There is the usual bit of biography:

> One week she only past in pain and woe,

and the usual vision of heaven:

> So with her Children four, she's now a rest,
> All freed from grief (I trust) among the blest.

The poem ends with the same gentle concept of God, who through all his afflictions is working for the benefit of his children, that we have found in the letters of the notebook.

> Chear up, (dear Son) thy fainting bleeding heart,
> In him alone, that caused all this smart;
> What though thy strokes full sad & grievous be,
> He knows it is the best for thee and me.

Thus in the four elegies we may trace the conflict of Flesh and
Spirit as it applies to the deaths of loved ones. The conflict is
more severe than in the loss of her possessions. In the elegies
on Elizabeth and Simon, feeling, or Flesh, brings the poet
almost to the point of criticising the methods of God, by
contrasting her proper statements with God's lack of con-
sideraton. In the poems on Anne and Mercy Bradstreet, the
Spirit wins with its rational religious arguments. And in the
poem on Mercy, her last poem, she resigns herself to affliction
as an evidence of God's concern.

The poem which begins "As weary pilgrim, now at rest,"
and titled "A Pilgrim" in the Harvard manuscript, is the last
poem outside the funeral elegies known to have been written
by Mrs. Bradstreet. It is dated August 31, 1669, and occupies
the last leaf of the notebook in which she wrote her
Meditations Divine and morall. Like the *Meditations,* it is in
Mrs. Bradstreet's own handwriting, and like the verses on the
burning of her house, it is in iambic tetrameter couplets. The
meter has a marked rhythm and an on-rushing quality that is
accented by the fact that the second line of the couplet most
frequently is not capitalized.

The first part of the poem is a simile, in which Anne
Bradstreet compares herself to a pilgrim who has passed
through danger and travail and has at last come to the end of a
long pilgrimage. For the first time she contemplates the care
without the joy of this world. The world of nature, which but a
few years before had shone so gloriously in "Contemplations,"
has now become a place of briars and thorns, stumps and
rocks, burning sun, storms and rains, hungry wolves and
erring paths. Some of the imagery is reminiscent of the elegy
on her father, as is the tone of acceptance and the hope of
heaven, for now she, as he, had spent her time on earth.[5] Both
were pilgrims who had come to the end of a long earthly span.
Of her father she had said:

> Upon the earth he did not build his nest,
> But as a Pilgrim, what he had, possest.

She depicts her own pilgrimage in similar terms:

> As weary pilgrim, now at rest,
>   Hugs with delight his silent nest
> His wasted limbes, now lye full soft
>   That myrie steps, have troden oft . . .

The second part of the poem, which turns to the resurrection
to come, derives from the tradition of the epithalamium or
wedding song as it was adapted to represent the union of
Christ with his church or with the human soul. The infusion of
this wedding song into Christian usage came through the Can-
ticle of Solomon and the Forty-fifth Psalm. Both of these were
probably epithalamia for human marriages, but from the time
of Origen they were interpreted as descriptions of the mystical
union of Christ and Church. The interpretation continued
through many medieval commentaries into the Reformation,
and is frequently found in New England sermons and other
writing. Anne Bradstreet in "A Pilgrim" uses several common
motifs of the epithalamium: the bed of death becomes a wed-
ding bed which "Christ did perfume"; the raiment of the bride
is described as the "glorious body" that will be "cloth'd upon"
the "Corrupt Carcasse." In recognition of the reunion of the
soul and the glorious body, there shall be "lasting joyes." A
characteristic call to the bridegroom occurs in the final ad-
dress to Christ: "then Come deare bridgrome Come away."[6]

The poem thus falls into two parts, one developing the tac-
tile images of a pilgrim overcome with weariness, the other
depending on the tradition of the wedding song to show the
glorious resurrection of the weary body. Even here, however,
Anne Bradstreet keeps close to the concrete and visible, or at
least tangible. The trials she describes the pilgrim undergoing
are trials of the body rather than the soul — the feeling of
wasted limbs, moving under a burning sun and stormy rains;
the galling of briars, thorns, rugged stones and stumps; the
menace of wolves; the eating of wild fruit instead of bread, and
the losing of the path. These images are of course used
metaphorically, but it perhaps does show the weariness of the
pilgrim that almost for the first time in her poetry she looks
with distaste upon the phenomena of the visible world. Until
the last twelve lines the poem speaks of despair with the world

coupled with desire for the respite of death. But in the last lines, Anne Bradstreet, accepting the desirability of the invisible, makes it once more a refreshing new, almost worldly, experience. The flesh will be donned once more as a new and glorious garment and death itself will be a marriage to an eternal bridegroom.

With this poem on her own expectancy of death and with the four elegies, the last of which is Anne Bradstreet's last dated poem, she has come full circle from her early poems, which were in expectation of death or funeral elegies. The contrast between the early and the late elegies brings out sharply the change we have heretofore been able only gradually to note in Anne Bradstreet's work.

The early elegies and the other poems of the 1630's and early 1640's are full of the gusto, the love of life, and the attempt to embrace large bodies of learning and experience that characterize the Renaissance. They are sensitive to ideas, personalities, and events of the contemporary scene or the recent past. They indicate a delight in learning, a pleasure in the reading of history, and a strong feeling of involvement in current political events. And they indicate a sensuous pleasure in the events of daily life, of the love of a husband and family, and the rural scene around her.

In style too, the early poems reflect the literary world she knew. There are the metaphysical conceits and images of the love poems; the elaborate metaphors of the early elegies; and the conception of the world in terms of dramatic interplay, of historical narrative, or, even, in the more personal poems, in terms of rhetorical argument. There is frequent use of the device of contrasting high and homely language and metaphor.

In contrast, the later poems are meditative and egocentric, concerned with the problems of the individual Christian in her search for God and in her resistance to God. These poems are still concerned with the world, but the concern represents the temptations of the flesh. The scene is internal, or, where the scene is external, it is shown as emblematic of Christian truths. The poet and the poet's reactions become important, in a way foreshadowed in the early work only in the poem written before the birth of a child. This shift of the poet to the foreground is slight if compared to the stance of a Romantic such as Wordsworth, but it is a move in that direction.

With the turning to more meditative poems, comes the development of a simpler and more direct style, a style more free of the use of conceit and extended metaphor. Direct statement or simile, or, at the most, metaphor that has several points of resemblance between tenor and vehicle, are the commonest methods of this period. There is also more variation in line length and rhyme pattern in the later poems.

But despite the changing of content and style, certain characteristics recur throughout the poet's work. First is the use of dramatic form. It appears as actual dialogue or monologue in the quaternions and "The Flesh and the Spirit." It occurs in implied fashion in "The Prologue" where the poet states the arguments against the writing of women and replies to them. The dramatic interplay of interior argument enlivens the poem on the burning of her house and the final elegies. In some poems she presents a scene, as in "The Author to her Book," where the poet speaks to the book and describes her efforts to improve it. Similarly, in "Contemplations" she places herself in the landscape and reacts to it, a technique used by certain other meditative poets, Vaughan, for example.

Another characteristic of her career is independence of mind. This appears in the early elegies and is notable in "The Prologue." It comes out in the notebook where she expresses her thoughts about God, takes the best position she can, and concludes "if I perish, I perish." Out of such independence grows another quality that has been noted again and again in these pages, the tension between feeling and statement, between dogma and her own humanity. The poems which lack both this tension and the resultant dramatic impetus are her weakest, notably the "Four Monarchies" and the poems of affliction and thanksgiving. In the poems to her husband and the family poems, especially the elegies on her grandchildren, she came close to committing the error that God warns about in Herbert's poem:

> He would adore my gifts in stead of r~e,
> And rest in Nature, not the God of Nature,

a doctrinal error into which a humane and sensitive personality is most apt to fall.

It was on a note of reconciliation to the decrees of God that the poetic career of Anne Bradstreet came to an end. Had the little elegy on Simon not intervened, we could have traced a continuing movement toward the reconciliation of feeling and doctrine in these last poems. In the poem on her house, she attempts to reconcile herself to the loss of her possessions by the use of reason. In the late elegies she tries to reconcile herself to the death of loved ones on the rational level, and at times also on the level of feeling. In "A Pilgrim" she considers the destruction of the flesh itself. And in this poem, Flesh has already lost out; there is no internal conflict. Only the inconveniences of the flesh are considered:

> This body shall in silence sleep
>   Mine eyes no more shall ever weep
> No fainting fits shall me assaile
>   nor grinding paines my body fraile
> With cares and fears ne'r cumbred be
>   Nor losses know, nor sorrowes see.

There is joyous acceptance of the promise of immortality:

> What tho my flesh shall there consume
>   it is the bed Christ did perfume
> And when a few yeares shall be gone
>   this mortall shall be cloth'd upon
> A corrupt Carcasse downe it lyes
>   a glorious body it shall rise
> In weaknes and dishonour sowne
>   in power 'tis rais'd by Christ alone
> Then soule and body shall unite
>   and of their maker have the sight
> Such lasting joyes shall there behold
>   as eare ne're heard nor tongue e'er told.

In the end the Spirit wins because it can outlast the Flesh, and the individual submits to the loss of the flesh and the hope of resurrection because she must. But even in this last event, the world to come is a more glorious version of this world. We are reminded of Anne Bradstreet's feeling when she first "came into this Country," where she "found a new world and new manners, at which" her "heart rose. But after" she "was convinced it was the way of God," she "submitted to it and joined to the church at Boston." Anne Bradstreet was always willing to submit to the inevitable during her long pilgrimage, but she did it only after using the full faculties of the mind and soul — the imagination, the affections, and the will — and it is the interplay that enlivens her poetry, this clash of feeling and submission that keeps it fresh today.

AFTERWORD

Anne Bradstreet died on September 16, 1672. John Norton, who had graduated from Harvard College the year before, wrote an elaborate funeral elegy in which he said:

> Praise her who list, yet he shall be a debtor
> For Art ne're feign'd, nor Nature fram'd a better.
> Her virtues were so great, that they do raise
> A work to trouble fame, astonish praise.
> When as her Name doth but salute the ear,
> Men think that they perfections abstract hear.
> Her breast was a brave Pallace, a *Broad-street,*
> Where all heroick ample thoughts did meet,
> Where nature such a Tenement had tane,
> That others souls, to hers, dwelt in a lane.

In 1678 the first American edition of her poetry was published under the title *Several Poems Compiled with great variety of Wit and Learning* . . . . The printer was John Foster, who two or three years earlier had set up the first printing press in Boston. Anne Bradstreet had begun revisions of her poems after the publication of *The Tenth Muse,* and she added to the poems of the first edition the elegies on her father and mother, the long poem "Contemplations," the dialogue of "The Flesh and the Spirit," and the witty little poem called "The Author to her Book." The title page announced this as "The second Edition, Corrected by the Author."

The book also had an editor — John Rogers, a physician, later President of Harvard College.[1] John Rogers had been a small boy when his father Nathaniel Rogers succeeded Nathaniel Ward as pastor of Ipswich church in 1636. No doubt he knew Mistress Bradstreet while he was growing up, and he married Anne Bradstreet's niece, the daughter of

Patience Dudley and Major-General Daniel Denison, who
were also residents of Ipswich. Rogers added his own poems of
praise for its author to the 1678 edition along with the com-
mendatory verses which had prefaced *The Tenth Muse*. Adop-
ting her "Contemplations" stanza for his tribute, after "sink-
ing in a sea of bliss," he records:

> Thus weltring in delight, my virgin mind
> Admits a rape; truth still lyes undiscri'd,
> Its singular, that plural seem'd, I find,
> 'Twas Fancies glass alone that multipli'd;
> Nature with Art so closely did combine,
> I thought I saw the Muses trebble trine,
> Which proved your lonely Muse, superiour to the nine.[2]

This last thought, especially, should have pleased the poet
whom the Muses once drove from Parnassus. No doubt
Rogers' special ties to the Dudley family enabled him also to
add to the American edition a number of personal poems not
contained in the earlier book, among them Anne Bradstreet's
poems to her husband, and the elegies on her grandchildren
and daughter-in-law, poems that are among her best. These
were preceded by the explanation: "Several other Poems made
by the Author upon Diverse Occasions, were found among her
Papers after her Death, which she never meant should come to
publick view; amongst which, these following (at the desire of
some friends that knew her well) are here inserted." Eighty
years later, in 1758, the second edition was reprinted in
Boston. Other poems — the poems of the notebooks, the poem
on the burning of her house, and "A Pilgrim"—remained un-
published until John Harvard Ellis edited *The Works of Anne
Bradstreet* in 1867.

In that same edition Ellis published for the first time Anne
Bradstreet's prose *Meditations* and the journal of religious ex-
periences written for her children. The simplicity, candor, and
expression of religious faith, together with the wisdom drawn
from practical experience in this world, appealed to the
readers of Ellis' book, and the prose of the *Meditations* and

journal for many years overshadowed the very real merits of the poetry.[3] Our own age, however, has come to value her first of all as a poet. Scholars, beginning with Charles William Pearson in 1908,[4] have viewed her work with increasing appreciation, to which several foremost poets have added their accolades. In 1929 Conrad Aiken attempted a revaluation of American poetry that would set her work above such favorites as Lowell, Longfellow, and Bryant;[5] Adrienne Rich praised the poet in the "Foreword" to Jeannine Hensley's edition of Bradstreet's *Works*; and John Berryman dedicated to Mistress Bradstreet his *Homage*.[6]   In 1930 the historian Samuel Eliot Morison called Bradstreet "a poet *sub specie aeternitatis*," a view close to that of the poet's own time. Cotton Mather, as well as Norton and Rogers, accorded her high praise. In the biography of Thomas Dudley in the *Magnalia* (1702) Mather wrote:

> But when I mention the *Poetry* of this Gentleman as one of his Accomplishments, I must not leave unmentioned the Fame with which the *Poems* of one descended from him have been Celebrated in both *Englands*. If the rare Learning of a *Daughter*, was not the least of those bright things that adorn'd no less a Judge of *England* than Sir *Thomas More*; it must now be said, that a Judge of *New-England*, namely, *Thomas Dudley*, Esq.; had a *Daughter* (besides other Children) to be a *Crown* unto him. Reader, *America* justly admires the Learned Women of the other *Hemisphere*... But she now prays, that into such Catalogues of Authoresses, as *Beverovicius*, *Hottinger* and *Voetius*, have given unto the World, there may be a room now given unto Madam Ann Bradstreet, the Daughter of our Governour *Dudley*, and the Consort of our Governour *Bradstreet*, whose *Poems*, divers times Printed, have afforded a grateful Entertainment unto the Ingenious, and a Monument for her Memory beyond the Stateliest *Marbles*.

No marble marks the burial place of Anne Bradstreet; there is no stone bearing her name in the graveyard at Andover, or on her father's tomb at Roxbury. Wherever the reluctant pilgrim came to rest at last, it was to become part of the earth of the New World, far from her native Lincolnshire. But even there she received a measure of the worldly fame she so desired. The fourteenth-century church of St. Botolph's at Boston in Lincolnshire, in which John Cotton preached and in which Thomas Dudley and his family often attended services, is one of the largest and finest parishes in England. It has the loftiest church tower in the country. It is a colorful church, with a gilded and painted ceiling and ornate interior decoration. Much of the missing stained glass has been replaced in recent years, including a series of windows containing lay figures.

Worked into the glass of one of these is a representation of John Cotton preaching to the Puritans who are about to embark on the *Arbella* for the voyage to America. Above the panel rise four large figures of women of Lincolnshire who have become famous in history. They are Anne of Bohemia, wife of Richard II; Margaret Beaufort, mother of Henry VII; Jean Ingelow, the poet, and Anne Bradstreet. Her portrait shows a young woman in Puritan dress holding a nest of birds. In brightness and stained glass, in the company of saints and queens, in one of the most colorful churches of England, Anne Bradstreet, the Puritan, has returned to her native land.

A CHRONOLOGY OF
THE WORKS OF ANNE BRADSTREET

The dates represent probable time of completion of the work. Where the works are undated, I have listed them in the most probable location, taking into account the statements in the work and external circumstances. Such dates are followed by (?). The place of first publication of each work is indicated after its title as follows:

(TM)   *The Tenth Muse*, London, 1650.

(SP)   *Several Poems*, Boston, 1678, as revised by Anne Bradstreet.

(SPA)   *Several Poems*, Boston 1678. From the sections of personal poems which Bradstreet's editor included though they had been omitted by their author.

(E)   *The Works of Anne Bradstreet in Prose and Verse*, ed. John Harvard Ellis, Charlestown, Mass., 1867.

Date Completed		
Mar. 25, 1632- Mar. 24, 1633	Upon a Fit of Sickness, *Anno.* 1632	(SPA)
1638-1639	An Elegie Upon that Honourable and renowned Knight, Sir *Philip Sidney* . . . 1638	(TM)
1641-1642	In honour of Du Bartas. 1641	(TM)
Mar. 20, 1642	To her most Honoured Father *Thomas Dudley* Esq . . .	(TM)
Mar. 20, 1642	The Foure Elements	(TM)
Mar. 20, 1642	Of the foure Humours in Mans constitution	(TM)

Mar. 20, 1642 or slightly later	The Four Ages of Man	(TM)
Mar. 20, 1642 or or slightly later	The four Seasons of the Yeare	(TM)
Aut. 1642- Mar. 24, 1643	A Dialogue between Old *England* and New . . .	(TM)
End of Dec., 1643	An Epitaph *On . . . Mrs. Dorothy Dudley who deceased* Decemb. 27. 1643 . . .	(SP)
1643-1647 ?	The Foure Monarchies . . .	(TM)
1640-1652 ?	Before the Birth of one of her Children	(SPA)
1641-1643 ?	To my Dear and loving Husband	(SPA)
1641-1643 ?	A Letter to her Husband, absent upon Publick employment	(SPA)
1641-1643 ?	Another	(SPA)
1641-1643 ?	Another	(SPA)
1647-1648 ?	Of the vanity of all worldly creatures	(TM)
1649 ?	*Davids* Lamentation for *Saul*, and *Jonathan*	(TM)
Before 1653	To her Father with some verses	(SPA)
Ca. Aug. 1, 1653	*To the Memory of . . . Thomas Dudley* Esq; *Who deceased*, July 31, 1653 . . .	(SP)
Spr. 1656 ?	To my Dear Children (prose)	(E)
Spr. 1656 ?	"By night when others soundly slept"	(E)
Spr. 1656 ?	For Deliverance from a feaver	(E)
Spr. 1656 ?	From another sore Fitt	(E)
Spr. 1656 ?	Deliverance from a fitt of Fainting	(E)
Spr. 1656	Meditations when my Soul hath been refreshed . . . (prose)	(E)
July 8, 1656	"I had a sore fitt of fainting . . ." (prose)	
Sum. 1656	"What God is like to him I serve"	(E)
Sum. 1656	"My soul rejoice thou in thy God"	(E)
Aug. 28, 1656	"After much weaknes and sicknes . . ." (prose)	(E)
May 11, 1657	"I had a sore sicknes . . ." (prose)	(E)
May 13, 1657	"As spring the winter doth succeed"	(E)
Sept. 30, 1657	"It pleased God to viset me . . ." (prose)	(E)
Ca. Nov. 6, 1657	Upon my Son Samuel his goeing for England, Novemb. 6, 1657	(E)
1659	In reference to her Children . . .	(SPA)

May 11, 1661	"It hath pleased God to give me ..." (prose)	(E)
May-June, 1661	"My thankfull heart with glorying Tongue"	(E)
June, 1661	For the restoration of my dear Husband ...	(E)
Ca. July 17, 1661	On my Sons Return out of England, July 17, 1661	(E)
Ca. Jan. 16, 1662	Upon my ... husband his goeing into England, Jan. 16, 1661	(E)
Jan-Sept., 1662	In my Solitary houres ...	(E)
Jan-Sept., 1662	In thankfull acknowledgment for the letters ...	(E)
Ca. Sept. 3, 1662	In thankfull Remembrance for my dear husbands safe Arrivall Sept. 3, 1662	(E)
1660-1670 ?	The Flesh and the Spirit	(SP)
Mar. 20, 1664-1672?	Meditations Divine and morall (begun 1664) (prose)	(E)
1664-1665 ?	Contemplations	(SP)
Aug., 1665	In memory of ... Elizabeth Bradstreet, who deceased August, 1665 ...	(SPA)
Ca. July, 1666	Verses upon the burning of our house, July 10th, 1666	(E)
1650-1670 ?	The Author to her Book	(SP)
1666-1670 ?	An Apology (follows *The four Monarchyes*)	(SP)
Ca. Nov. 16, 1669	In memory of ... Anne Bradstreet	(SPA)
Aug. 31, 1669	"As weary pilgrim, now at rest"	(E)
Ca. Nov. 16, 1669	On ... Simon Bradstreet, Who dyed on 16. Novemb. 1669	(SPA)
Ca. Sept. 6, 1670	To the memory of ... Mercy Bradstreet	(SPA)

Vidit cuncta quæ fecerat   et erant valde bona. gen.1.31.

יהוה

D·IACOBO·MAGNÆ·BRITANNIÆ·   FR·ET·HIBERNIÆ·REGI·SACRVM·

DU
BARTAS
HIS
Diuine WEEKES,
And WORKES
with
A Compleate Collectiō
of all the other moſt
delight-full WORKES.
Translated and
written by ŷ
famous
Philomuſus,
IOSVAH SYLVESTER
Gent:

Iob
Triumphant

R·EIſtracke ſculpſit   LONDON printed by
Robert Young with
Additions 1641:

Title page of Joshua Sylvester's translation of Du Bartas with panels illustrating stories
from the Bible.

PASSAGES FROM ANNE BRADSTREET
RELATED TO PASSAGES FROM
JOSHUA SYLVESTER

Sylvester

From Elegy on William Sidney:
Although I know none, but a Sidney's Muse,
Worthy to sing a Sidney's Worthinesse.

Arcadians know no Other, for Apollo,
No other Mars (in Arms or Arts to follow

But more peculiar, and precisely mine;
Lineally bound unto that Noble Line.

Next, His son Philip (more than Philip's Son)
Whose World of Worth, a World of Honour won

That All men once (as well as Low, the High,
Of either sex, of every sort) must dye.

From Elegy on Mrs. Hill:
Her April past, her Summer-Age prepares

. . . .
His [Du Bartas'] love and labour apted so my wit,
That when Urania after rapted it,
Through Heav'ns strong working weaknesse did produce
Leaves of delight, and fruits of sacred use.

From Elegy on William Sidney:
Whose memory, on Muses fairest Hill
Is canonized, by a Phoenix Quill.

From Dedication to James I:
As when th' Arabian (only) bird doth burne
Her aged body in sweet flames to death
Out of her cindars a new bird hath breath
In whom the beauties of the first returne
Of our dead Phoenix (dear Elizabeth)

From Dedication to "Honour's Fare-well":
Receive, conceive, consider This Direction
Against th' Excesse, the Rage, The Insurrection
Of Tears, of Sighs, of Sorrowes for This Dame
As Dead, Who Lives (In Soule, in Seed, in Fame)
    etc.

From Elegy on Prince Henry:
His goodly body shall more glorious rise.

Of sobbing words a Sable Webbe to weave.

Bradstreet

From Elegy on Sidney:
And makes me now with Sylvester confesse,
But Sydney's Muse, can sing his worthinesse.

Mars and Minerva did in one agree,
Of Armes, and Arts, thou should'st a patterne be.

Let then, none dis-allow of these my straines,
Which have the self-same blood yet in my veines.

O Princely Philip, rather Alexander,
Who wert of honours band, the chief Commander.

Thus man is borne to dye, and dead is he

From Elegy on Du Bartas:

A homely flour in this my latter Spring,
If Summer, or my Autumn age do yield,
Flours, fruits, in Garden, Orchard, or in Field

From Elegy on Elizabeth:

No Phoenix pen, nor Spensers poetry

She was a Phoenix Queen, so shall she be,
Her ashes not reviv'd, more Phoenix she.

She wrackt, she sackt, she sunk his Armado.

(NOTE: Use of triple lists in these passages)

From "A Pilgrim":
A glorious body it shall rise.
From Elegy on Sidney:
His death present in sable to his wife.

Frontispiece from George Wither's *A Collection of Emblemes*, 1635, with emblematic figures of good and evil.

IMAGES IN THE POETRY
FREQUENCY LIST

(Prepared by Rose Shade)

Note: These line counts do not include poems in which the entire poem refers to one of these subjects.

1.	THE HUMAN BODY	522
2.	ILLNESSES AND DEATH	238
3.	NATURE — FLORA	209
4.	BIBLICAL	171
5.	FAMILY RELATIONSHIPS	161
6.	NATURE — FAUNA	157
7.	CLASSICAL	151
8.	NATURE— THE HEAVENS	147
9.	WARFARE	125
10.	OCCUPATIONS (GENERAL)	114
11.	RICHES, METALS, GEMS	104
12.	NATURE— THE EARTH	85
13.	ROYALTY	79
14.	NATURE — SEASONS/WEATHER	74
15.	HISTORY	63
16.	GEOGRAPHY	50
17.	COLORS	42
18.	MUSIC	40
19.	TEMPERATURE*	36
20.	POETRY	36
21.	NATURE — THE SEA	35
22.	CLOTHING	34
23.	HOUSEHOLD ITEMS	21
24.	CATHOLICISM*	21
25.	FLIGHT*	18

26. SINGING*   14
27. TOOLS*   14
28. FINANCE AND LEGAL*   13
29. THE HUMOURS**   12
30. TIME   11
31. TOUCH*   9
32. IMPERMANENT EARTH   8
33. NAUTICAL   7
34. SOUNDS*   7
35. KNOT   7
36. WINE AND DRINKING   6
37. PROCREATION*   5
38. BUBBLES   5
39. TASTE*   4
40. MISC: BOTTLES, AGE,
    ALMS, A FAIR,
    HUNTING.

TOTALS OF MAIN CATEGORIES:

THE HUMAN BODY   955
Includes the body, illness and
death, the family, and clothing.

NATURE   708
Includes flora, fauna, the
heavens, the earth, seasons and
weather, and the sea.

OCCUPATIONS   400
Includes royalty, warfare, poetry,
nautical and music.

* Images found all in one poem
** Does not include poem "The Four Humours."

BOOKS WITH WHICH
ANNE BRADSTREET WAS ACQUAINTED

John Harvard Ellis in *The Works of Anne Bradstreet in Prose and Verse* (Charleston, Mass., 1867; reprinted Gloucester, Mass., 1962), pp. xvi-xx, mentions writers who were prominent during the early seventeenth century. Elizabeth Wade White in *Anne Bradstreet "The Tenth Muse"* (New York, 1971), pp. 60-70, discussing the author's early education, lists books that she may have encountered. White also includes (pp. 386-390) the inventory of books in the library of Anne Bradstreet's father, Thomas Dudley, at the time of his death. Adrienne Rich in the "Foreword" to *The Works of Anne Bradstreet*, edited by Jeannine Hensley (Cambridge, 1967), p.xi, also gives a brief list of books Bradstreet may have read. The following table summarizes the evidence which these and other sources, as well as the present study, give for presuming Bradstreet's acquaintance with each book or author listed.

RELIGIOUS WORKS

The Bible and Holy Scriptures Conteyned in The Olde and Newe Testament. Translated According to the Ebrue and Greke . . . With moste profitable annotations upon all the hard places, and other things of great importance . . . , 1560.
The Geneva Bible, favored by Puritans. 150 editions between 1560 and 1644. References to the Bible and paraphrases of Biblical passages are found throughout Bradstreet's work. Among the longer paraphrases are "David's Lamentation for Saul and Jonathan" (2 Sam. 1.19); the last part of "Old Age" (1 Chron. 12.8; Cant. 2.9 and 17; Eccl. 12.1-8); and the conclusion of "A Dialogue between Old England and New" (Zech. 14.20-21). Additional citations may be found in the notes to the editions of Bradstreet's *Works,* edited by Ellis and by Hensley,

and in *Poems of Anne Bradstreet* edited by Robert
Hutchinson (New York, 1969).

The Psalms of David in Meter.
   The Sternhold and Hopkins versions of the metrical
Psalms appeared in numerous editions after Sternhold's
first publication of nineteen Psalms in 1540. With
additional translations by others, all 150 Psalms were
attached to the *Book of Common Prayer* in 1562 and
were used for singing by the congregation. See the
discussion of the influence of the metrical psalms on
Bradstreet's first extant poem in "Part I: The Ipswich
Poems" and on her later devotional poetry in Chapter 7.

*The Whole Book of Psalmes Faithfully Translated into
English Metre*, 1640.
   "The Bay Psalm Book," used after its publication in 1640
for singing by the congregations of the Bay Colony. See
Chapter 7; also Josephine Piercy, *Anne Bradstreet* (New
Haven, 1965), pp.79-81.

SERMONS

Stephen Marshall. *Meroz Curse*, 1642.
   See the discussion in Chapter 4.

William Hooke. *New Englands Teares, For Old Englands
Feares*, 1641.
   See the discussion in Chapter 4.

PHYSIOLOGY

Helkiah Crooke, M.D. *Microcosmographia or a Description
of the Body of Man*, 1615.
   Bradstreet mentions *"curious, learned Crooke"* (line 568,
"Of the four Humours"). See the discussion in Chapter 3,
"The Four Humours." Helen McMahon gives a table of
parallel passages between this work and "Of the Four
Humours" in "Anne Bradstreet, Jean Bertault, and Dr.
Crooke," *Early American Literature* III (Fall, 1968), pp.
118-119.

HISTORIES

Sir Walter Raleigh. *The History of the World*, 1614.
    Though Bradstreet mentions Raleigh by name only twice in "The Four Monarchies" (in the section on Artaxerxes Mnemon in "The Persian Monarchy" and in that on Darius Codomanus in "The Persian Monarchy," (first edition only), her poem is largely a condensation in the form of verse paraphrase of this author. Her first four lines describing the golden age are drawn from Raleigh, Book I, Ch. IX, Section III; then she moves to the story of Nimrod in Ch. X, Section I ff. The passages in which she finds her material are easy to trace. Parallel passages exemplifying her method occur in Ellis (pp. xliv-xlix), White (pp. 235-236), and Piercy (pp. 30-31).

The Lives of the Noble Grecians and Romanes . . . By that Grave Learned Philosopher and Historiographer Plutarke of Chaeronea, Translated out of Greeke into French by James Amyot: and out of French into Englishe by Thomas North, 1579.
    Bradstreet refers to Plutarch by name twice in "The Four Monarchies," in the section on Artaxerxes Mnemon (Ellis, p. 246), and later in the section on Aridaeus, where she recommends *The Lives* to anyone wishing to learn more than she tells about Aridaeus. Ellis (xlix-l) quotes a passage from Plutarch which Bradstreet added to her account of Alexander in the second edition (pp. 283-284). Since the references to Plutarch above are all found in the second edition only, Ellis concludes that she read Plutarch after she had completed the first version of the poem. White (pp. 67-68), however, finds a parallel between Plutarch and the lines that begin "The Roman Monarchy" in both editions and contends that Bradstreet was familiar with Plutarch at the time of the original writing.

John Speed. *Historie of Great Britaine under the Conquests of the Romans, Saxons, Danes, and Normans from Julius Caesar, to our most gracious Soveraigne, King James*, 1611.

Bradstreet refers to Speed's history in the elegy on Queen Elizabeth (line 20). See Chapter 4, note 1. Ellis notes that she probably derived some of the facts in "A Dialogue between Old England and New-England" from Speed.

William Camden. *Annales or The History of the Most Renowned and Victorious Princess Elizabeth*. Translated by R. Norton, 1630.

Bradstreet refers to Camden in the elegy on Elizabeth (l. 20) and he may be one source for her catalog of the glories of the reign in that poem.

William Pemble. *Period of the Persian Monarchie*, 1631.

She refers to Pemble in the description of Darius Codomanus at the conclusion of "The Persian Monarchy" as if familiar with his book, saying "Thus learned *Pemble*, whom we may not slight"; the entire passage is changed in the second edition and the reference to Pemble is omitted.

Richard Knolles. *The Generall Historie of the Turkes*, 1603.

A copy of this book was in Thomas Dudley's library. Ellis quotes parallel passages from "The Four Seasons" and Knolles' account of Bajazet (pp. 173-174).

Archbishop James Usher. *Annals of the World,* 1658.

Bradstreet apparently used this book in revising "The Four Monarchies." She refers to him once by name in the section on Ninias in "The Assyrian Monarchy."

Sir John Temple. *History of the Irish Rebellion*, 1646.

See Chapter 4.

John Foxe. *Actes and Monuments*, 1563.

Nowhere does Bradstreet refer to Foxe or his book by name. However, in the letter to her children (Ellis, p. 9) she mentions the Papists' "cruell persecutions of the Saints, which admitt were they as they terme them, yet not so to bee dealt withall." She may be referring here to the bloodshed in Ireland or to the martyrdoms depicted by Foxe. White (p.64) mentions this book as one of the religious writings that "had a part in the upbringing of every well-taught nonconformist child." The book was popular with other Anglicans as well as with the Puritan reformers.

LITERATURE

Joshua Sylvester. *Du Bartas His Divine Weekes and Works, with a Compleate Collection of all the other most delight-full Workes Translated and written by that famous Philomusus Joshua Sylvester, Gent.*, 1621.

See Chapter 1 and the table of "Passages from Anne Bradstreet Related to Passages from Joshua Sylvester." References to Du Bartas, in addition to those in the elegies, occur in "The Prologue" (ll. 8 and 11) and in "To Her Most Honoured Father" which precedes the quaternions (l. 34). Her name is coupled with that of Du Bartas throughout the poem by Nathaniel Ward and in an anagram, both prefacing *The Tenth Muse.* Imagery in Du Bartas' "The Fifth Day" is generally conceded to be the source of Bradstreet's use of the Dove and the Mullet in "As loving Hind"; see parallel passages in Alessandra Contenti "Anne Bradstreet, il Petrarchismo e il 'Plain Style,' " *Studi Americani*, XIV (1968), 21-22. Contenti (pp.20-21) also cites a passage in Du Bartas that contains groups of images related to those in stanzas 8, 9, 21, and 26 of "Contemplations." Helen McMahon, (*supra,* pp. 118-119) gives a number of parallels between Bradstreet's "Four Humours" and the "Panaretus" of Jean Bertault, also translated by Sylvester and in this 1621 edition.

Edmund Spenser. *The Faerie Queene* (including 'Two Cantos of Mutabilitie"), 1609.

Bradstreet mentions Spenser twice. Lines 19-22 of the elegy on Queen Elizabeth read:

No Phoenix pen, nor Spencers poetry,
No Speeds nor Cambdens learned History
Elizahs works, warrs, praise, can e're compact,
The World's the Theatre where she did act.

Later in the poem she refers to Elizabeth as a "Phoenix Queen." When she revised the Sidney elegy for the second edition, she removed her references to Stella and added a reference to Spenser's *Astrophel* (ll.61-64), this time calling the poet "Phoenix Spenser." The first of these quotations appears to refer to *The Faerie Queene*, which, no more than the histories of Elizabeth's reign, can fully describe her glories. Spenser is closely allied with the name of the Queen through the use of "Phoenix" (which incidentally alliterates with "Faerie") as an epithet for both. Spenser is called "Phoenix" because he wrote about the "Phoenix Queen" who continued to live in his verses as Sidney lived also. See Dorothea Kehler "Anne Bradstreet and Spenser," *American Notes & Queries*, VIII (1970) 135, for a parallel between stanzas 31-32 of "Contemplations" and Book I, Canto III, stanza 30 of *The Faerie Queene*. See also the discussion of the influence of the *Cantos of Mutabilitie* in the section on "The Four Seasons" in Chapter 3.

The Shepheardes Calender, 1579.
See the comparison of "The Author to her Book" to Spenser's "To His Booke" in Chapter 6. White (p. 268) also notes the parallel.

Colin Clouts Come Home Again, 1595.
This volume contains *Astrophel*. See Chapter 2; also note that the "hartless deare" of line 9 of *Colin Clouts Come Home Again* may be echoed in Bradstreet's "As loving Hind that (Hartless) wants her Deer."

Fowre Hymnes, 1596.
Piercy (p. 89) compares lines 101-104 of Bradstreet's "The Flesh and the Spirit" to lines 11-14 of "An Hymne in Honour of Beauty."

All of the above volumes were brought together in the editions of Spenser's works of 1611 and 1617, and Bradstreet may have read Spenser in one of these rather than in separate volumes. Taken altogether the passages cited, together with her references to Spenser, indicate a considerable assimilation of Spenser's writing, enough to offset the disclaimer of T. G. Hahn in "Urian Oakes's *Elegie* on Thomas Shepard and Puritan Poetics," *American Literature*, XLV (1973), p. 171 n.

Sir Philip Sidney, *Astrophel and Stella,* 1591.
See the discussion of Bradstreet's elegy on Sidney in Chapter 1. In the first edition of the Sidney elegy she devotes lines 71-92 to the Stella of this sonnet series, indicating a familiarity with its story. These lines were removed in the second edition and were replaced by a reference to Spenser's *Astrophel.* Piercy (p. 87) suggests that Sonnets 89 to 100 may have influenced Bradstreet's love poems to her husband.

The Countess of Pembrokes Arcadia, 1590.
Bradstreet devotes nineteen lines of her elegy on Sidney (ll. 14-32) to praise of this book. Sidney is apparently the "noble, brave Archadian" of lines 25-28 in "Summer" in "The Four Seasons"; these lines appeared in the first edition, but were expunged in the second. Bradstreet also probably refers to Sidney in the first twenty-eight lines of "Youth" in "The Four Ages"; see the discussion in Chapter 3 and note 24. Piercy (p. 123, n. 28) suggests a comparison between "As Weary Pilgrim" and Plangus' lament in Sidney's *Arcadia.*

William Shakespeare.
Caution should be observed in claiming any large influence of Shakespeare on Bradstreet. Hans Galinsky in "Anne Bradstreet, Du Bartas und Shakespeare in Zusammenhang kolonialer Verpflanzung und Umformung europaischer Literatur" (*Festschrift fur Walther Fischer*, Heidelberg, 1959, pp. 145-180) was the first to suggest the possibility, but his comments are inconclusive. Josephine Piercy (pp. 59-61, 87, 95) presents the case most fully. She sees Bradstreet's use of a "stage" as she introduces the four Ages and as Old Age enters, as

a parallel to the speech of Jacques in *As You Like It*. But the use of "stage" can be attributed at least in part to the need for a rhyme for "age." Also the term was used, as Piercy states, several times in Sylvester's book, which we know Bradstreet read carefully. The use of four ages was a common figure in the time. So too with other metaphors which Piercy introduces, as "withering age" and "Serjeant Death's Arrests." Death is described twice in Du Bartas as a Serjeant and once carries a "sad warrant" (White, pp. 64-65). "Death's arrest" is found in Wilson (see below); so Bradstreet need not have gone to Hamlet for this familiar figure. Here again she needed a rhyme word for "breasts."

Piercy (p.61) compares the fate of Bradstreet's Calisthenes who "lov'd his master more than did the rest,/ As did appear, in flattering him the least" in "The Grecian Monarchy" to that of Cordelia in *King Lear*. But Bradstreet's lines are drawn directly from Raleigh's description of him as "a man of free speech, honest, learned, and a lover of the king's honour" "who would never condescend to betray the king to himself, as all his detestable flatterers did" and needs no dependence on Shakespeare's tale of Cordelia. Moreover, the story of Cordelia is told in Holinshed's *Chronicles* (Chaps. V and VI) and in Spenser's *Faerie Queene* (II.X.27-32), as well as other sources. However, Rose Shade, who prepared the "Table of Images" for this study, finds a further likeness. She reports: "Images of Finance and Legal terms predominate in one poem, 'To Her Father with Some Verses, telling of the 'debt' she owes her father. This poem is also interesting in the echoes of Shakespeare's *King Lear* that it seems to hold. When Bradstreet speaks of the 'bond' which 'remains in force' and which no one can discharge but she, we are reminded of Cordelia in the first act of *Lear* when she says 'I love your majesty/ According to my bond; nor more nor less.' Before that, Cordelia has replied to his demands for flattery that she has 'nothing' to say. Lear says 'nothing will come of nothing.' In this poem the line 'Where nothing's to be had Kings loose their right' seems a reflection of the scene in *Lear*."

The case for a Shakespearean influence on Bradstreet rests then at present largely on the use of the term "stage" in combination with Four Ages; Bradstreet's use of the phrases "Serjeant Death's Arrests," "withering age," and "buds new blown, to have so short a date," (regarding this last figure see Chapter 10, n. 3 and White, pp. 351-352) and one or two other common images of the period, and a parallel with the situation of Cordelia in *King Lear*. This is not much evidence of a strong Shakespearean influence. However, perhaps because Piercy has argued the case for Shakespearean influence at length, the idea of a strong influence has gotten into the literature on Bradstreet. Alvin H. Rosenfeld in his generally well researched essay on "Contemplations" (cited in Chapter 9, note 12) states, without further proof, that Shakespeare "was one of Anne Bradstreet's favorite authors." However, his comment that her treatment of time and oblivion in the last stanza of "Contemplations" recalls some of Shakespeare's sonnets and his noting the use of the couplet in this one stanza are both well taken. Perhaps he had in mind especially Sonnet 55 "Not marble, nor the gilded monuments," which, though it is not mentioned specifically by Piercy either, is probably the closest of the Shakespearean sonnets to this stanza.

In sum, at present we have only a few tantalizing small parallels to indicate a Shakespearean influence on Bradstreet. These may indicate at most that she was acquainted with some of the sonnets (perhaps through exchanges of copied versions with friends) and that she may have read passages from some of the plays. Until further parallels come to light, this is all we can say with assurance.

Francis Quarles. *Sions Sonets. Sung by Solomon the King, And Periphras'd by Fra. Quarles*, 1625.

Quarles was popular with Puritans; moreover, he was in

touch with some of the leaders of the Massachusetts Bay
Colony. In 1638 he sent them some of his translations of
the Psalms (Ellis, p. xviii). *Sions Sonets* are a series of
eight-line stanzas, rhyming in couplets, in the form of a
dialog between the Bridegroom and the Bride. The Bride
speaks of "the Sunne-like face" of the Bridegroom. This
and other imagery suggests that in Bradstreet's poems to
her husband. Alessandra Contenti ("Anne Bradstreet, il
Petrarchismo e il 'Plain Style,' " *Studi Americani*, XIV
(1968), 24-25) quotes some passages containing similar
imagery.

Emblemes and Hieroglyphikes, 1639.
  See the discussion of a possible influence on "The Flesh
  and the Spirit" (Chapter 7) and on "Contemplations"
  (Chapter 8). Contenti (p.23) also notes the influence of
  Quarles in providing an example of post-Spenserian
  stanzas.

Enchiridion, 1641.
  These prose aphorisms may be a source for Bradstreet's
  Meditations.

John Wilson. *A Song, or Story, For the Lasting Remem-
brance of diverse famous works, which God hath done in our
time*, 1626.
  White, pp. 122-123, claims that Bradstreet read this poem
  of her fellow-colonist. She quotes a stanza which uses the
  figure, "deaths arrest" similar to Bradstreet's "Serjeant
  Death's arrests" (Youth" l. 88, first edition only).

Virgil. *The Aeneid*.
  Bradstreet deliberately echoes the opening lines of the
  Aeneid at the beginning of her "Prologue." How much
  she knew of the rest of the book is not clear. She refers to
  Dido in lines 77-78 of the elegy on Queen Elizabeth.

Miscellaneous Poems in Anthologies or Commonplace Books
  Such as those of John Donne (see Chapter 2, and note 6;
  also Piercy p. 87); Robert Southwell (see Chapter 2 and
  note 6); and Robert Herrick (see Piercy, p. 123, note 28).

SELECTED BIBLIOGRAPHY
OF WORKS BY AND ABOUT
ANNE BRADSTREET

Editions

The Tenth Muse Lately sprung up in America. Or Severall Poems, compiled with great variety of Wit and Learning, full of delight. Wherein especially is contained a compleat discourse and description of The Four Elements, Constitutions, Ages of Man, Seasons of the Year. Together with an Exact Epitomie of the Four Monarchies, viz. The Assyrian, Persian, Grecian, Roman. Also a Dialogue between Old England and New, concerning the late troubles. With divers other pleasant and serious Poems. By a Gentlewoman in those parts. Printed at London for Stephen Bowtell at the signe of the Bible in Popes Head-Alley. 1650.

Several Poems Compiled with great variety of Wit and Learning, full of Delight; Wherein especially is contained a compleat Discourse, and Description of The Four Elements. Constitutions, Ages of Man, Seasons of the Year. Together with an exact Epitome of the three first Monarchyes Viz. The Assyrian, Persian, Grecian. And beginning of the Romane Common-wealth to the end of their last King: With diverse other pleasant & serious Poems, By a Gentlewoman in New-England. The second Edition, Corrected by the Author, and enlarged by an Addition of several other Poems found amongst her Papers after her Death. Boston, Printed by John Foster, 1678. [Ed. John Rogers.]

Several Poems Compiled with great Variety of Wit and Learning, full of Delight; Wherein especially is contained, a compleat Discourse and Description of The Four Elements, Constitutions, Ages of Man, Seasons of the Year. Together with an exact Epitome of the three first

145

Monarchies, viz. the Assyrian, Persian, Grecian, and Roman Common Wealth, from its beginning, to the End of their last King. With divers other pleasant and serious Poems. By a Gentlewoman in New-England. The Third Edition, corrected by the Author, and enlarged by an Addition of several other Poems found amongst her Papers after her Death. Re-printed from the second Edition in the Year M.DCC.LVIII. [Boston: no publisher given.]

The Works of Anne Bradstreet in Prose and Verse, ed. John Harvard Ellis. Charlestown [Mass.] : Abram E. Cutter, 1867. Reprinted, New York: Peter Smith, 1932; Gloucester Mass.: Peter Smith, 1962.

The Poems of Mrs. Anne Bradstreet (1612-1672). Together with Her Prose Remains with an Introduction by Charles Eliot Norton. [Ed. Frank E. Hopkins.] [New York?:] The Duodecimos, 1897.

A Dialogue Between Old England and New, and Other Poems. Old South Leaflets, General Series, VII, No. 159. Boston: Directors of the Old South Work, 1905.

The Tenth Muse (1650) and, From the Manuscripts, Meditations Divine and Morall Together with Letters and Occasional Pieces by Anne Bradstreet, ed. Josephine K. Piercy. Gainesville, Florida: Scholars' Facsimiles & Reprints, 1965.

The Works of Anne Bradstreet, ed. Jeannine Hensley. Cambridge, Mass.: Belknap Press of Harvard University Press, 1967.

Poems of Anne Bradstreet, ed. Robert Hutchinson. New York: Dover Publications, Inc., 1969.

Scholarship and Criticism since 1930

The following comprise the most important essays and books on Anne Bradstreet in recent years. For a more complete list, including commentary before 1930 from both scholarly and general sources, see my "Anne Bradstreet: An Annotated Checklist," *Bulletin of Bibliography* XXVII (1970), 34-37.

Morison, Samuel Eliot. "Mistress Anne Bradstreet," *Builders of the Bay Colony*. Boston and New York, 1930. Pp. 320-336.

Vancura Zdenek. "Baroque Prose in America," *Studies in English by Members of the English Seminar of the Charles University, Prague*, IV (1933), 35-58.

Svendsen, J. Kester. "Anne Bradstreet in England: A Bibliographical Note," *American Literature*, XIII (Mar. 1941), 63-65.

Whicher, George Frisbie. *Alas, All's Vanity, or, A Leaf from the First American Edition of Several Poems by Anne Bradstreet*. New York, 1942.

Jantz, Harold S. "First Century of New England Verse," *American Antiquarian Society Proceedings*, LIII, N.S. (Oct. 1943), 252-254.

Richardson, Lyon N. "Bradstreet, Anne," *Dictionary of American Biography*, II (1943), 577-578.

Crowder, Richard. "Phoenix Spenser: A Note on Anne Bradstreet." *New England Quarterl;y*, XVII (June, 1944), 310.

White, Elizabeth Wade. "The Tenth Muse — A Tercentenary Appraisal of Anne Bradstreet," *William and Mary Quarterly*, VIII (July, 1951), 355-377.

Charles, Buchanan. "Colonial Manuscript Back Home," *Library Journal*, LXXXI (Jan. 15, 1956), 148-149.

Crowder, Richard. "Anne Bradstreet and Keats," *Notes and Queries*, CCI (Sept. 1956), 386-388).

Peltola, Niilo. *The Compound Epithet and Its Use in American Poetry from Bradstreet through Whitman*. (Annales Academiae Scientiarum Fennicae. Ser. B, 105.) Helsinki, 1956.

Warren, Austin. "The Puritan Poets," *New England Saints.* Ann Arbor, 1956. pp. 7-14.

Galinsky, Hans. "Anne Bradstreet, Du Bartas und Shakespeare im Zusammenhang kolonialer Verpflanzung und Umformung europaischer Literatur: Ein Forschungsbericht und eine Hypothese," *Festschrift fur Walther Fischer.* Heidelberg, 1959. Pp. 145-180.

Fuess, Claude M. "Andover's Anne Bradstreet, Puritan Poet," *Andover Symbol of New England.* Andover Historical Society and North Andover Historical Society, 1959.

Eby, Cecil D., Jr. "Anne Bradstreet and Thomas Gray: A Note on Influence," *Essex Institute Historical Collections,* XCVII (1961), 292-293.

Hensley, Jeannine. "The Editor of Anne Bradstreet's *Several Poems,*" *American Literature,* XXXV (1964), 502-504.

Piercy, Josephine K. *Anne Bradstreet.* New Haven, 1965.

Stanford, Ann. "Anne Bradstreet as a Meditative Writer," *California English Journal,* II (Winter, 1966), 24-31.

―――. "Anne Bradstreet: Dogmatist and Rebel," *New England Quarterly,* XXXIX (1966), 373-389.

―――. "Anne Bradstreet's Portrait of Sir Philip Sidney," *Early American Literature Newsletter,* I (Winter, 1966-67), 11-13.

Richardson, Robert D. "The Puritan Poetry of Anne Bradstreet," *Texas Studies in Literature and Language,* IX (1967), 317-331.

Contenti, Alessandra. "Anne Bradstreet, il Petrarchismo e il 'Plain Style,' " *Studi Americani,* XIV (1968), 7-27.

Johnston, Thomas E., Jr. "A Note on the Voices of Anne Bradstreet, Edward Taylor, Roger Williams, and Philip Pain," *Early American Literature,* III (1968-1969), 125-126.

McMahon, Helen. "Anne Bradstreet, Jean Bertault, and Dr. Crooke," *Early American Literature*, III (1968-1969), 118-123.

Kehler, Dorothea. "Anne Bradstreet and Spenser," *American Notes & Queries*, VIII (1970), 135.

Laughlin, Rosemary M. "Anne Bradstreet: Poet in Search of Form," *American Literature*, XLII (1970), 1-17

Rosenfeld, Alvin H. "Anne Bradstreet's 'Contemplations': Patterns of Form and Meaning," *New England Quarterly*, XLIII (1970), 79-96.

Hildebrand, Anne. "Anne Bradstreet's Quaternions and 'Contemplations,' " *Early American Literature*, VIII (1973), 117-125.

Requa, Kenneth A. "Anne Bradstreet's Poetic Voices," *Early American Literature,* IX (1974), 3-18.

Eberwein, Jane Donahue. "The 'Unrefined Ore' of Anne Bradstreet's Quaternions," *Early American Literature,* IX (1974), 19-26.

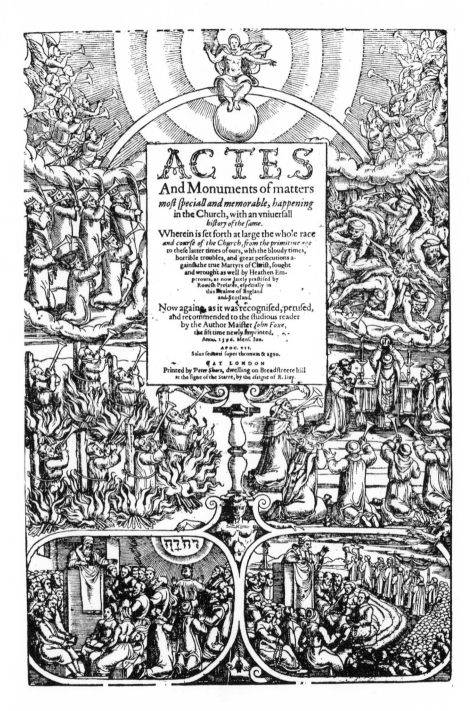

Title page of John Foxe's *Actes and Monuments*, the *Book of Martyrs*.

FOOTNOTES

INTRODUCTION

1. Sources for the ancestry and life of Anne Bradstreet are: [Cotton Mather], "The Life of Mr. Thomas Dudley," *Massachusetts Historical Society Proceedings*, XI (1869-70), 207-222; Augustine Jones, *Thomas Dudley, Second Governor of Massachusetts*, (Boston, 1899); John Harvard Ellis, "Introduction," *The Works of Anne Bradstreet in Prose and Verse* (Charlestown, Mass., 1867; reprinted, Gloucester, Mass., 1962); Elizabeth Wade White *Anne Bradstreet: "The Tenth Muse"* (New York, 1971).

2. In her elegy on Du Bartas Anne Bradstreet so describes a fair such as she may have seen in Boston, Lincolnshire. See *The Works of Anne Bradstreet in Prose and Verse*, ed. John Harvard Ellis (Charlestown, Mass., 1867), p.354.

3. A. M. Cook, *Lincolnshire Links with the U.S.A.* (Lincoln, Lincs., 1956), pp.37, 40. Canon Cook in conversation disclosed that he believes the Earl's house to have been located on Little Bargate Street, near the location of the old town gate.

4. White, p. 54.

5. On Frances Wray, Countess of Warwick, see White, pp. 77-78; Ann Stanford, "Anne Bradstreet's Portrait of Sir Philip Sidney," *Early American Literature Newsletter* I, no. 3 (Winter 1966-67), 12.

6. Edward Hyde, Earl of Clarendon, *The History of the Rebellion and Civil Wars in England* (Oxford, 1849) I, 255.

7. John Gorham Palfrey, *A Compendious History of New England* (Boston, 1873), I, 106.

8. John Knox Laughton, ed., *State Papers Relating to the Defeat of the Spanish Armada*, Navy Records Society, I (London, 1894), 308. His son is stated to have "belonged to a puritan family." *Dict. Nat. Biog.*, s.v. "Rich, Robert, second Earl of Warwick."

9. *Dict. Nat. Biog.*, s.v. "Rich, Robert, second Earl of Warwick."

10. Jones, pp. 35-36; White, pp. 79-89.

11. *Letter to the Countess of Lincoln* in *Chronicles of the First Planters of . . . Massachusetts Bay, 1623-1636*, ed. Alexander Young (Boston, 1846), p. 311.

12. *The Charlestown Records*, Young, p. 378.

13. Dudley, *Letter to the Countess of Lincoln*, Young, p. 310.

14. *Works*, ed. Ellis, p.5.

15. *New England's Prospect* (London, 1634), p. 39. Also in Young, p.402.

16. *Bradford's History of Plymouth Plantation*, ed. William T. Davis (New York, 1908), ·p. 96.

17. The Puritan vision of life has had a continuing fascination for scholars. Important books on the subject range from such classics as William Haller's *The Rise of Puritanism* (New York, 1938) and Perry Miller's *The New England Mind: The Seventeenth Century* (Cambridge, 1954) to such recent works as Darrett B. Rutman's *American Puritanism* (Philadelphia, 1970) and Stephen Foster's *Their Solitary Way: The Puritan Social Ethic in the First Century of Settlement in New England* (New Haven, 1971).

PART I: THE IPSWICH POEMS

1. Samuel Eliot Morison, *Builders of the Bay Colony* (Boston and New York, 1930), pp. 223, 271.

2. "Helluo Librorum." Cotton Mather, *Magnalia Christi Americana* (London, 1702), Book 2, p. 17.

CHAPTER 1

1. The fact that Anne Bradstreet changed the second of these lines to "Whilst English blood yet runs within my veins," in the second edition, has been taken by her editor Ellis to be a retraction of her claim to kinship with Sidney. Augustine Jones in *The Life and Work of Thomas Dudley* (Boston and New York, 1899), pp. 3-7, gives a full discussion of Thomas Dudley's belief in the relationship to Sidney and argues that Anne Bradstreet changed the line as a matter of decorum. Elizabeth Wade White in *Anne Bradstreet: "The Tenth Muse"* (New York, 1971) pp. 7-30 gives the most thorough account of the Dudley family and agrees with Jones on the reason for the change. More than decorum was probably involved in the change, however. See the discussion of the elegy on Thomas Dudley in Chapter 9.

2. The poet herself must have been aware of this problem, for she simplified the alternation in the second edition.

3. A. L. Bennett in "The Principal Rhetorical Conventions in the Renaissance Personal Elegy," *Studies in Philology*, LI (1954), pp.

107-126, finds that during the Renaissance "the writing of memorial verses on the death of great men became a literary fashion." He describes the new type as a "personal, non-pastoral lament." Its chief features are praise of the deceased and consolation for the bereaved; sometimes the poet's chief purpose was to write "a panegyric rather than a lament." Such elegies, according to Bennett, followed the pattern given in numerous Renaissance rhetorics for praise of a person under the places of birth, childhood, adolescence, manhood, old age, and death, or under the four virtues of prudence, justice, courage, and temperance.

Anne Bradstreet, though her purpose was praise, did not follow the pattern of the lament as outlined by Bennett. Nor did she follow entirely the devices of the pastoral elegy. Sylvester's memorial poems, however, follow more closely the type described by Bennett, though he seems conscious also of the devices of pastoral elegy.

4. An example of such a belated tribute is *A Chaine of Pearle; or, a Memoriall of the Peerles Graces and heroick vertues of Queene Elizabeth, of glorious memory. Composed by the Noble Lady Diana Primrose* (London, 1630). The poem eulogizes the late Queen under the "Pearls" of the ten virtues. Its author, described as "the *Prime-Rose* of the *Muses* nine" in an introductory poem, like Anne Bradstreet compares Elizabeth to a Sun and says that her glories "doe the greatest Princes dampe" and deserve to be described by "Apollo's quill.".

5. In the second edition the last line reads: "That *Sidney* dy'd 'mong most renown'd of men."

CHAPTER 2

1. First edition. In the second edition, Anne Bradstreet omits her extended comparison of Stella to a comet which portends ill for Sidney. It is not clear exactly what she considers their relationship within the sonnet series to be. In the second edition, in which she refers for the first time to Spenser's *Astrophel*, she follows Spenser in referring to Stella as Sidney's wife. See my discussion in "Anne Bradstreet's Portrait of Sir Philip Sidney," *Early American Literature Newsletter*, I, 3 (1966-1967), 11-13.

2. For a full discussion, see Edmund S. Morgan, *The Puritan Family* (New York, 1966).

3. Herbert J. C. Grierson, *Cross-Currents in 17th Century English Literature* (New York, 1958), p. 59. "Spenser is doctrinally a Puritan because, like Wither and Milton ... he seeks the realization of the Good in love, not with Plato in the realm of the abstract Idea of Beauty, but in a perfect wife."

4. Thomas Wilson discusses the three kinds of orations in *The Arte of Rhetorique* (1553), reprinted several times during the latter half of the sixteenth century.

5. "What differentiates the conceits of the metaphysicals is not the fact that they very frequently employ curious learning in their comparisons . . . It is the use which they make of the conceit and the rigorous nature of their conceits, springing from the use to which they are put, which is more important than their frequently learned content. A metaphysical conceit . . . is not indulged in for its own sake. It is used . . . to persuade, or it is used to define, or to prove a point." Helen Gardner ed., *The Metaphysical Poets* (London, 1957), p. 20.

6. To give just a few examples, exaggerated tear imagery is found in Robert Southwell's "The Burning Babe," John Donne's "Twicknam Garden," and in "The mourning Muse of Thestylis" one of the poems in *Astrophel*, Spenser's collection of poems written by himself and others on the death of Sidney. Since Anne Bradstreet was probably acquainted with this work, the tear imagery may be of especial interest:

> her eies a lake
> Of teares had bene, they flow'd so plenteously therefro.
>
> (ll. 125-126)
>
> *Aurora* halfe so faire, her selfe did never show,
> When from old *Tithons* bed, shee weeping did arise.
> The blinded archer-boy, like larke in showre of raine
> Sat bathing of his wings, and glad the time did spend
> Under those cristall drops, which fell from her faire eies.
>
> (ll. 132-136)
>
> All things with her to weep, it seemed, did encline,
> The trees, the hills, the dales, the caves, the stones so cold.
> The aire did help them mourne, with dark clouds, raine and
>   mist.
>
> (ll. 143-145)

7. This time range seems appropriate to these poems for several reasons: she specifically mentions being at Ipswich; her reference to "fruits" indicates she has at least two children; the metaphysical imagery is closest to her earlier — pre-1650 — style.

8. Morgan, pp. 48-50.

9. Rosemund Tuve in *Elizabethan and Metaphysical Imagery* (Chicago, 1947) p. 102, speaks of the comparison of a woman to a bird as a simile "whose logical simplicity holds the reader to one obvious likeness," and which "mutes the string because overtones are not desired." Thus this type of image may be differentiated from the metaphysical conceit, which stresses the unlikeness as an overtone.

10. Anne Bradstreet is here using a paraphrase of Hebrews 11:4 in which Abel by faith "being dead yet speaketh." This phrase, according to Harrison T. Meserole, was often used by Puritan

writers to justify the publication of works not to gain worldly fame, but for the "fame in heaven" of Milton's *Lycidas*.

CHAPTER 3

1. For the second edition, she made several changes in this letter to indicate the added quaternions.

2. *Du Bartas His Divine Weekes and Workes*, trans. by Joshua Sylvester (London, 1621), p. 32 (Second Day of the First Week). Anne Bradstreet uses the same parallels as Du Bartas, except that instead of aligning infancy with fire, choler, and summer, she supplies Manhood; and she gives Childhood to water, phlegm, and winter.

3. Helen McMahon was the first to suggest this source. See "Anne Bradstreet, Jean Bertault, and Dr. Crooke," *Early American Literature* III (Fall, 1968), 118-119.

4. McMahon, p. 118, also notes the pattern of "charge and countercharge" in this poem.

5. E. M. W. Tillyard, *The Elizabethan World Picture* (London, 1943), pp. 55-59. See also Francis R. Johnson, *Astronomical Thought in Renaissance England* (Baltimore, 1937).

6. Du Bartas, p. 26 (Second Day.) McMahon notes the similarity between Bradstreet's conclusion and that of Bertault's "Panaretus," where the virtues, having ceased to quarrel, form a ring around the Prince.

7. Du Bartas, p.76 (Fourth Day).

8. Perry Miller, *The New England Mind: The Seventeenth Century* (Cambridge, Mass., 1954), p. 216. "The employment of Nature as symbol or as doctrine was . . . more important than the choice of which particular system of physics was used to explain nature . . . there was only incidental concern about whether the universe were expounded according to the old or the new astronomy."

9. Du Bartas, p. 204, describes Adam's state after the fall in "The Furies," the third part of the "First Day of the Second Week." Not only is Adam, but the whole world affected. "In brief, the whole scope this round Centre hath,/ Is a true store-house of Heav'ns righteous wrath."

10. Tillyard, p. 63.

11. (London, 1651), p.99.

12. Crooke, p. 699, defines bones according to Galen as "the hardest, the dryest, and most terrestriale parts of the creature."

13. Tillyard, pp. 63-64.

14. Crooke, p. 100.

15. Crooke, p. 474.

16. Crooke, p. 2. "The Soul of Man is but one, yet that one consisting of three Essentiall and distinct Faculties or Powers, intellectuale, sensitive and vegetative."

17. Helen McMahon *op. cit.,* pp. 120-122, has found a passage parallel to this quotation in Dr. Crooke, p. 3: "Why should I presume to describe the Essence of the Soul, seeing it partaketh of so much Divinity . . . the Soul of Man is wholly in the whole, and wholly in every particular part." McMahon cites numerous other parallel passages in Bradstreet's "Four Humours" and Dr. Crooke's *Microcosmographia.*

18. Crooke, p. 17.

19. Evert A. and George L. Duyckinck, *The Cyclopaedia of American Literature* (New York, 1855), I, 48.

20. Tillyard, p. 57.

21. Lily B. Campbell, *Shakespeare's Tragic Heroes* (New York, 1952), p. 58.

22. Tillyard, p. 65.

23. *The Works of Anne Bradstreet in Prose and Verse*, ed. John Harvard Ellis (Charlestown, Mass., 1867), p. 1 [50].

24. Ann Stanford, "Anne Bradstreet's Portrait of Sir Philip Sidney," *Early American Literature Newsletter* I (Winter 1966-1967) 11-13.

25. Gwendolen Murphy, ed., *A Cabinet of Characters* (London, 1925), p. xxix.

26. In the second edition, Anne Bradstreet takes note of the changing fashion and refers to powdered wigs in the first two lines:

If time from leud Companions I can spare,
'Tis spent to curle, and pounce my new-bought hair.

27. Harold S. Jantz, *The First Century of New England Verse* (New York, 1962), p. 37. Jantz comments "the section on "Old Age" . . . is obviously a versification of personal reminiscences and political attitudes of her father."

28. The use of this and other literary conventions of her time has led to numerous comments such as that regarding her "stiffness of style" (Charles Francis Richardson, *A Primer of American Literature*, Boston 1878, pp. 14-15); the drawing of illustrations "from the old outworn literary stock" (Charles Eliot Norton, "Introduction," *The Poems of Mrs. Anne Bradstreet Together with Her Prose Remains*, New York, 1897, p. ix); and to the regret that she followed the conceitists rather than having more passion and imagination (Ernest Erwin Leisy, *American Literature*, New York, 1929, pp. 13-14).

29. The word "Almonds" has been substituted in this passage for "Medlar" which occurred in the first edition. The Medlar is a small

tree much cultivated in Europe; The fruit resembles a crab apple and is used for preserves. The change to "Almonds" in the second edition may indicate a deliberate effort to make the autumn more exotic.

30. Wine, raisins of the sun, almonds, figs, and oranges are among the imports listed as coming into New England in the last half of the century. Among the items shipped by John Hull in his vessels were wines and fruits from Spain. George Francis Dow, *Every Day Life in the Massachusetts Bay Colony* (Boston, 1935), pp. 151-152.

31. Jantz, p. 37, states that her references to nature portray the English rather than the American countryside, especially the one on autumn. But the passage quoted is the only description of scenery in "Autumn."

32. On the figure of amplification, see Rosemond Tuve, *Elizabethan and Metaphysical Imagery* (Chicago, 1947), pp. 90, 92.

33. Duyckinck, I, 48.

34. Samuel Eliot Morison, *Builders of the Bay Colony* (Boston and New York, 1930), pp. 331-332.

CHAPTER 4

1. John Speed, whose *Historie of Great Britaine under the Conquests of the Romans, Saxons, Danes and Normans* (London, 1611) she mentions in another poem, devotes a section of his book to these invasions, and also follows the pattern of contention for the throne which she develops in the first few pages of the "Dialogue."

2. C. V. Wedgewood, *The King's War* (New York, 1959), p.80.

3. *Dict. Nat. Biog.*, s.v. "Marshall, Stephen."

4. Raymond Phineas Stearns, *The Strenuous Puritan: Hugh Peter* (Urbana, Ill., 1954), describes the activities of the colonial agent in England.

5. Temple reported that 300,000 were killed on both sides in two years of rebellion. Other accounts contain other estimates of the number killed. The use by Anne Bradstreet of Temple's figure indicates she relied on his *History*. Temple was an important source for James Anthony Froude's *The English in Ireland in the Eighteenth Century*. Thomas Fitzpatrick in *The Bloody Bridge and other Papers Relating to the Insurrection of 1641* (Dublin, 1903) p. ix, claims that "the alleged 'Massacre' — the Massacre of Milton, Temple, Borlase, May, Rushworth, Cox, Harris, Carlyle, and Froude — is a stupendous falsehood, even on the showing of the very documents which the charge is, ignorantly or malignantly, based, namely, the Depositions preserved in Trinity College, Dublin."

6. Bradstreet has a long passage describing Old England's sins (ll. 89-145). It begins with a brief catalog of terms similar to those used by Hooke. She says:

Before I tell th' Effect, I'le shew the Cause
Which are my sins the breach of sacred Laws,
Idolatry supplanter of a Nation,
With foolish Superstitious Adoration,
Are lik'd and countenanc'd by men of might,
The Gospel troden down and hath no right:
Church Offices were sold and bought for gain,
That Pope had hope to find, *Rome* here again,
For Oaths and Blasphemies, did ever Ear,
From *Belzebub* himself such language hear.

Hooke says "And let us be every day confessing of our old *England* sinnes, of its high pride, Idolatry, superstition, blasphemies, blood, cruelties, Atheismes, &c." (p. 23).

Bradstreet, always pragmatic, adopts another argument also used by Hooke when she has *Old England* ask "If I decease, dost think thou shalt survive?/Or by my wasting state dost think to thrive?" Hooke says of England: "Thence hath the Lord thus stockt this American part with such Worthies . . . thence hitherto have been our yearely supplies of men, and of many an usefull commoditie. If then they suffer, we may easily smart; if they sink, wee are not likely to rise. And this, at least, may be a perswasive to a sordide minde, that will not be wrought upon by more ingenuous Arguments."

Bradstreet, like Hooke, also describes the horrors of war (ll. 193-199) though she does so much more briefly.

7. In the second edition Anne Bradstreet changed "Prelates" to "Popelings," in accord with the new politics after the Restoration. Note here the poet's pun on the Root and Branch Petition.

8. *An Exposition upon The Thirteenth Chapter of the Revelation* (London, 1656), p. 50.

9. Anne Bradstreet was not alone among the women of her family in being unconventional. In 1646 her younger sister, Sarah, who had married Benjamin Keane, evoked the following comment from Stephen Winthrop in London: "My she Cosin Keane is growne a great preacher." Later that year Sarah was admonished by the church in Boston for "irregular prophesying" and the next year was excommunicated for the same offense. See Elizabeth Wade White, *Anne Bradstreet: "The Tenth Muse"* (New York, 1971) pp. 174-176.

CHAPTER 5

1. John Winthrop, *The History of New England from 1630 to 1649*, ed. James Savage (Boston, 1826), II, 216.

2. "The Prologue" differs in stanza form from all the rest of Anne Bradstreet's poetry. *The Tenth Muse* (1650), save for this poem and one other small exception, is in iambic pentameter

couplets. "The Prologue" is her first poem to be divided into definite stanzas. Its rhyme scheme, *ababcc*, is closest to the scheme Bradstreet used in "Contemplations." Possibly the stanza form here, like that of "Contemplations," was suggested by Francis Quarles' *Emblemes and Hieroglyphics*, 1639. Quarles uses iambic pentameter, rhyming *ababcc*, in several "Emblemes" (Book IV. 3 and 9; Book V. 6).

3. Elizabeth Wade White in *Anne Bradstreet: "The Tenth Muse"* (New York, 1971) pp. 238-241, suggests that "The Prologue" was written after "The Four Monarchies" to accompany the latter when the poet presented it to her family and friends. White thus places it after the move to Andover.

4. D. D., "Governor Thomas Dudley's Library," *New England Historical and Genealogical Register*, XII (October, 1858), pp. 355-356.

5. See John Harvard Ellis, *The Works of Anne Bradstreet in Prose and Verse* (Charlestown, Mass., 1867) pp. xliii-l, who quotes a number of passages from Raleigh and one from Plutarch that parallel lines in "The Four Monarchies."

CHAPTER 6

1. Cotton Mather, *Magnalia Christi Americana* (London, 1702) Book III, p. 219.

2. This early reference to Anne Bradstreet was discovered by Elizabeth Wade White, who cited it in "The Tenth Muse — A Tercentenary Appraisal of Anne Bradstreet," *William and Mary Quarterly*, VIII (1951) 366-367. White (pp. 372-377) discusses Anne Bradstreet's importance as a pioneer in the writing of serious poetry by women.

3. James Savage, "Gleanings for New England History," *Collections of the Massachusetts Historical Society*, XXVIII (1843), 295.

4. What Samuel Eliot Morison said of Anne Bradstreet's reactions to *The Tenth Muse* in *Builders of the Bay Colony* (Boston and New York, 1930), p. 331, is to a certain extent misleading:

> 'The Tenth Muse' did this for Anne Bradstreet: it completely cured her of the Du Bartas disease, and of writing imitative poetry. She was thirty-eight when the book came out in 1650. For the remaining twenty-two years of her life, she wrote lyrical poetry.

Anne Bradstreet's indebtedness to Du Bartas' subject matter was heaviest in "The Four Elements" (1642), and although she later used material gleaned from her reading of Du Bartas, she did not imitate him except in the first two quaternions. She never used metaphysical

conceits as extensively as Du Bartas did, and there was a gradual
movement in her style toward simpler, more open metaphors. The
most complicated metaphors are found in the love poems to her
husband, but these were not published in *The Tenth Muse*, and they
were more closely allied to the love poems of the English
metaphysical poets than to Du Bartas. Her "Four Monarchies" is
imitative in the sense that it draws on the subject matter of Raleigh,
and she did not stop work on "The Romane Monarchy" after the
publication of her book in 1650, but added to it until the manuscript
was burned in 1666.

She did turn to more personal subject matter after 1650, but she
was still following English forms — psalms, elegies, meditations. We
can certainly, with Morison, characterize these forms as more
"lyrical." However, her feeling about *The Tenth Muse* was not one
of rejection and realization that she had been wrong. The book, as
has been shown, was praised and appreciated, and Anne Bradstreet
herself worked on improving the details of the poems and correcting
errors of the printer — hardly signs of being "cured."

PART II: THE ANDOVER POEMS

1. *Mass. Colony Records*, I, p. 237, quoted in *Works*, p. xxxvi.

2. John Winthrop, *The History of New England from 1630 to
1649,* ed. James Savage (Boston, 1825), II, 85 (Sept. 22, 1642).

3. Winthrop, II, 195, 252-253.

4. Samuel Maverick, *A Briefe Discription of New England*
(Boston, 1885), p. 12.

5. Maverick, p. 11.

6. Edward Johnson, *Johnson's Wonder-Working Providence
1628-1651*, ed. J. Franklin Jameson (New York, 1910), p. 249.

7. *Works*, p. xxxvii.

8. Timothy Dwight, *Travels; in New-England and New-York*
(New Haven, 1821), I, 401.

9. Josephine K. Piercy comments on the resemblance of this
epitaph to a "character" in *Anne Bradstreet* (New York, 1965), p.
91.

10. Elizabeth Wade White, *Anne Bradstreet: "The Tenth Muse"*
(New York, 1971), pp. 246-248.

11. William Hooke, *New Englands Teares, for Old Englands
Feares* (London, 1641), p. 3.

CHAPTER 7

1. The poet recalls but three illnesses that occurred before the
notebook entries of 1656: (1) Before she was fourteen or fifteen she

had "a long fit of sickness" in which she was confined to bed. How long this childhood illness actually was — any illness is long to a child — there is no way to tell. (2) About sixteen, she had smallpox, a disease from which many people died in those times. She was strong enough to survive. (3) After coming to the new world she "fell into a lingering sickness like a consumption, together with a lameness." It is probably during this illness that she wrote her first dated poem "Upon a Fit of Sickness, *Anno*, 1632", perhaps after the second hard winter in this country. When we remember how many died during those first winters mere survival may be taken as a sign of health.

When she came to write the notebook of 1656-1657, a period of recurrent illness involving chills, fever, and weakness, she tried to recall previous sicknesses, and the above three are all those she considered serious enough to record. In the almost quarter-century between 1632 and 1656, between the ages of 19 and 44, she mentions no sickness, except for the twelve lines of iambic pentameter couplets entitled "Upon some distemper of body," which are undated and may have been written anytime. Significantly, this last poem breaks off at a semicolon, unfinished, as if its author recovered speedily. During the period 1633-1656, Anne Bradstreet bore eight children by natural childbirth; moreover, she raised them all to maturity and except for one, they outlived her. During January, 1661, after four years of good health as she tells us, the poet became ill and weak and remained so until mid-May, when she had a fever for four days, then recovered. During June of the same year Simon, her husband, certainly a healthy man, also had a fever, and Hannah, the Bradstreet's daughter, also had a fever in June or July. The poet records no further illness, living on to the age of sixty, a good ripe age for those times.

On balance, there are more signs of health than weakness in the constitution of Anne Bradstreet. A mere list of her activities during her life in America should convince us of her vigor. She and her family were pioneers, continually pressing against the frontier. She managed her household, directing or performing its many tasks; often she ran the family farm without the assistance of her husband, who was absent on public business. (For a partial list of activities required to maintain a farming household, see "The Four Seasons.") She attended long church services and lectures. She performed the duties of a magistrate's wife. And she produced a large body of poetry, much of it far surpassing the efforts of her New England contemporaries.

2. John Winthrop, *The History of New England from 1630 to 1649*, ed. James Savage (Boston, 1825), I, 58-59.

3. Winthrop, I, 67-68 (Nov. 23, Dec. 8, 1631).

4. In an excellent commentary on such later poems as "The Flesh and the Spirit" and "Contemplations," Robert D. Richardson, Jr., describes "Anne Bradstreet's struggles between love of this world and reliance on the next . . . not as the rebelliousness of an anti-Puritan temperament but as an attempt to achieve the Puritan ideal of living in the world without being of it." (*Texas Studies in Literature and Language*, IX (1967) 317-331).

CHAPTER 8

1. *The Works of Anne Bradstreet in Prose and Verse*, ed. John Harvard Ellis (Charlestown, Mass., 1867) p. 73 n.
2. Louis L. Martz, *The Poetry of Meditation* (New Haven, 1954), pp. 16-20, 153-154.
3. Martz, pp. 27-38.
4. Richard Baxter, *The Saints Everlasting Rest* (London, 1650), pp. 691, 731-747, 753-755.
5. St. Francois de Sales, *An Introduction to a Devoute Life*, 3d ed. (Rouen, 1614), p. 139. Quoted by Martz, p. 37.
6. Baxter, p. 761.
7. Thomas Shepard, quoted in Perry Miller, *The New England Mind: The Seventeenth Century* (Cambridge, Mass., 1954), p. 210.
8. "The Autobiography of Thomas Shepard," *Publications of the Colonial Society of Massachusetts*, XXVII (1930), 362.
9. See Rosemary Freeman, *English Emblem Books* (London, 1948).
10. Martz, p. 61 n. For an extensive discussion of the emblem in colonial New England see Alan B. Howard, "The World as Emblem: Language and Vision in the Poetry of Edward Taylor," *American Literature*, XLIV (1972), 359-384.
11. For example, Charles William Pearson, "Early American Poetry" in *Literary and Biographical Essays* (Boston, 1908), pp. 16-21.
12. Alvin H. Rosenfeld in "Anne Bradstreet's 'Contemplations': Patterns of Form and Meaning," *New England Quarterly* XLIII (1970), pp. 79-96, notes this inability, saying, "Her song *is* a song of praise, but she could only sing well what her imagination, and not her moral consciousness, responded to faithfully" (p. 89).
13. The tensions that exist within Bradstreet's later poetry have been frequently commented upon; several recent articles have added significantly to the discussion. Alvin H. Rosenfeld, cited above, traces the relationship of the poem to later Romanticism, showing the poet's resistance to Wordsworthian and Keatsian resolutions and her use of seasonal metaphor. Robert D. Richardson, Jr., in "The Puritan Poetry of Anne Bradstreet," *Texas Studies in Literature and*

Language, IX (1967), 317-331, sees in "Contemplations" a Puritan attempt "to achieve a balance between this world and the next."

14. See Josephine K. Piercy, "The Prose Writer" in *Anne Bradstreet* (New York, 1965), pp. 102-109, for a discussion of the development of Bradstreet's prose within the *Meditations.*

CHAPTER 9

1. Robert Henson, "Sorry After a Godly Manner: A Study of the Puritan Funeral Elegy in New England," Dissertation (University of California, Los Angeles, 1957) pp. 6-8, 32.

2. In the second edition she also dropped the passage in which she attempts to drive "Fame's flaming chariot." The voices which decried her claiming relationship to Sidney may also have criticized her attempt to sieze fame. Likewise she omitted her praise of "the noble, brave Archadian" (Sidney) in lines 25-28 of "Summer" in "The Four Seasons."

3. Some writers have quoted this line, among others, to suggest that Anne Bradstreet knew Shakespeare's sonnet which contains the line "And summer's lease hath all too short a date." See Hans Galinsky, "Anne Bradstreet, Du Bartas und Shakespeare im Zusammenhang kolonialer Verpflanzung und Umformung europaischer Literatur," *Festschrift fur Walther Fischer*,Heidelberg, 1959, pp. 145-80, and Josephine Piercy, *Anne Bradstreet* (New York, 1965), p. 95. Elizabeth Wade White, however, rejects the need for a source, saying that "this woman who had spent almost all her life with countryside around her did not have to be told by Shakespeare that early buds can be blasted by winter winds." *Anne Bradstreet: "The Tenth Muse"* (New York, 1971), p. 352. Those who suggest a possible influence of Shakespeare on Anne Bradstreet rely either on images found throughout late sixteenth and early seventeenth-century poetry and which actually occur in other sources we know she read (for example, Spenser's "Astrophel" (ll. 25-34) contains the image of the flower "untimely cropt"); or on rhyme words. English has so few good rhyme words that they must be used over and over and are not good indicators of influence.

4. Kenneth B. Murdock in "Writers of New England," in *Literary History of the United States*, ed. Robert E. Spiller, et al., (New York, 1963) p. 64, notes that in this poem "Anne Bradstreet realizes that she is perilously close to writing rebelliously against God's decrees. She pulls herself up in the last line."

5. The idea of writing a valedictory to the world in poetic form may have come to Anne Bradstreet indirectly from her father, Thomas Dudley, who left a farewell poem in his pocket when he died. It will be remembered that the poet herself had written a

farewell in 1632 when she thought she was near death, and again in the poem before the birth of a child. The possibility of a genre of valedictory poems is suggested by the fact that Edward Taylor wrote three valedictions; they are presented in Thomas M. Davis's "Edward Taylor's 'Valedictory' Poems," *Early American Literature*, VII (Spring, 1972), 38-63.

6. I am indebted to Professor Virginia Tufte of the University of Southern California for the suggestion that this poem uses the motifs of the epithalamium. See her *The Poetry of Marriage: The Epithalamium in Europe and Its Development in England*, University of Southern California Studies in Comparative Literature, Vol. II (Los Angeles, 1970).

AFTERWORD

1. Jeannine Hensley in "The Editor of Anne Bradstreet's *Several Poems*," *American Literature*, XXXV (1964), 502-504, produces the evidence for Rogers' editorship.

2. John Harvard Ellis, ed. *The Works of Anne Bradstreet in Prose and Verse* (Charlestown, Mass., 1867), p. 95.

3. This view is expressed in a review of Ellis's Book in *The North American Review*, CVI (Jan. 1868), 330-334; Moses Coit Tyler, *A History of American Literature During the Colonial Period, 1607-1765* (New York and London, 1878; reissued, Ithaca, New York, 1949), pp. 239-253; and Helen S. Campbell, *Anne Bradstreet and Her Time* (Boston, 1891).

4. "Early American Poetry," *Literary and Biographical Essays* (Boston, 1908), pp. 16-21. This is not to imply that recent critical comment has been entirely favorable to the poet. Roy Harvey Pearce, for example, finds Bradstreet lacking "a Puritan insistence on fixing once and for all the meaning of the event as that meaning is somehow bound up in a communal experience" (*The Continuity of American Poetry* (Princeton, 1961), p. 24.

5. Conrad Aiken, ed., *American Poetry 1671-1928* (New York, 1929).

6. *Homage to Mistress Bradstreet* (New York, 1956).

INDEX